THE BOOK OF
CHRISTMAS
FOODS

THE BOOK OF
CHRISTMAS
FOODS

JANICE MURFITT

Photographed by
PAUL GRATER

a Salamander book

Published by Salamander Books Limited
LONDON • NEW YORK

Published 1989 by Salamander Books Ltd.,
52 Bedford Row, London WC1R 4LR

This book was created by Merehurst Limited,
Ferry House, 51-57 Lacy Road, Putney, London SW15 1PR

© Salamander Books Ltd., 1989

ISBN: 0 86101 460 X

Commissioned and directed by Merehurst Limited
Managing Editor: Felicity Jackson
Editor: Louise Steele
Designer: Roger Daniels
Home Economist: Janice Murfitt
Photographer: Paul Grater
Typeset by Angel Graphics
Colour origination by Magnum Graphics Limited
Printed in Belgium by Proost International Book Production

Companion volumes of interest:

The Book of COCKTAILS
The Book of CHOCOLATES & PETITS FOURS
The Book of HORS D'OEUVRES
The Book of GARNISHES
The Book of PRESERVES
The Book of SAUCES
The Book of ICE CREAMS & SORBETS
The Book of GIFTS FROM THE PANTRY
The Book of PASTA
The Book of HOT & SPICY NIBBLES – DIPS – DISHES
The Book of CRÊPES & OMELETTES
The Book of PIZZAS & ITALIAN BREADS
The Book of SANDWICHES
The Book of GRILLING & BARBECUES
The Book of SOUPS
The Book of DRESSINGS & MARINADES
The Book of CURRIES & INDIAN FOODS

CONTENTS

INTRODUCTION

This book is devoted entirely to Christmas, packed with exciting ideas and wonderful recipes and planned to make Christmas a joy, not a chore. Each section of the book has a mixture of recipes suitable for all occasions and all members of the family – some quick and easy to make, others more advanced creative recipes.

Christmas Fare is the largest section, ranging from the old traditional favourite recipes with a difference – Christmas cakes, puddings, mince pies, roast turkey – as well as some delicious alternatives for those wishing to try something completely different: fruits, wine, nuts and herbs made into tasty stuffings, vegetables presented in different ways, pâtés and terrines suitable for a buffet party, quick lunch or supper, and many recipes using leftover food and offering quick and tempting dishes.

Other sections in this book include Canapés, offering tiny mouthfuls of tempting food made from a variety of cheeses, meat, fish, eggs or vegetables – all so pretty and quick to make, and may be served with a variety of drinks made from the drinks section.

As separate sections, Desserts & Puddings and Cakes & Biscuits have a good selection of simply delicious recipes, many of which may be made in advance or kept in the freezer until required. Try using different fruits than those suggested to ring the changes.

Gifts and Decorations are very special sections with recipes that do take a little longer but can be made in advance and stored for several weeks. The delicate sugar cards are a joy to make and to receive, or try making a festive bread ring, made to the design given in the recipe, or to your own design, to hang up with pretty ribbon, or place on the table as a centrepiece. The chocolates and sweets look so pretty when packed in tiny boxes and tied up with ribbon, and make a delightful gift for anyone, as do fruits in liqueurs, Spiced Citrus Slices, Brandied Mincemeat or Satsuma Pine Nut Conserve.

I do hope this book gives you pleasure in preparing your own gifts, decorations and Christmas fare.

— PLANNING CHRISTMAS FOOD —

Christmas is the most wonderful time of year when family and friends meet to celebrate this happy occasion. Everything seems to buzz with excitement as the festivities fill the air – and the time should be of happiness and giving.

However, so often as Christmas approaches, panic surrounds us and thoughts of how to plan the food; what to cook; how much to make and so on . . . fill our minds. *The Book of Christmas Foods* is designed to help answer these questions and includes all manner of recipes relating to the festive season from Traditional Christmas fare, such as the dinner and accompaniments, to cakes, puddings and mince pies, plus delicious alternatives and much, much more.

You will find simple recipes to make and freeze ahead of time; delicious desserts and puddings to impress your family and guests and a range of eyecatching canapés to serve with drinks or to make, in quantity, for a party. There's also a wonderful selection of cakes and biscuits which offers a range of lovely ideas, including some novelty ones for children. The drinks section

too, is sure to be popular with everyone as it caters for kiddies as well as adults: children will love to mix their own drinks, especially when they have friends to visit. And, last but not least there's a delightful selection of decorations and gifts to make ahead of time – which are fun to do and are sure to bring you compliments!

The Book of Christmas Foods has over 100 delicious recipes – each and every one illustrated with colourful and informative step-by-step photographs to guide you to success every time. Each recipe section has been planned to make Christmas much easier, simply by containing a selection of ideas to suit all occasions and help make Christmas a deliciously trouble-free, happy occasion.

The festive holiday spreads over several days and even into the New Year, so careful planning is the essence of success. Think ahead and plan the food required for each day of the holiday. Take into account the foods which will be left over, such as poultry, vegetables and fruit and select recipes to utilise these ingredients in the best

way. Spend some time cooking certain foods for the freezer to be prepared for those unexpected arrivals. Make a fish and meat pâté and freeze whole, or cut into slices (to thaw more quickly): served with a salad and crusty bread a pâté makes a delicious impromptu meal. Freeze a few puddings or gâteaux for impressive desserts. Frozen finger foods also make marvellous standbys and certainly take the pressure out of entertaining at short notice: made so tiny, these tempting 'bites' offer so much and produce a tasty selection of foods to serve with drinks.

Once you have planned the menus and decided how many visitors are expected, work out which recipes may be made in advance – either to freeze or store until required, such as Christmas cakes, puddings and mince pies. And, if you've time, even fit in a few edible decorations and home-made gifts which will keep, to help ease the pressure later on. Make a detailed shopping list of food to be purchased in advance and also for last-minute shopping. And stock up on drinks and ingredients for nibbles several weeks

before to avoid the last minute rush in the days leading up to Christmas.

Try to make Christmas Eve part of the celebrations instead of spending the time up to the early hours of the morning stuffing the turkey! Why not allow some time to wrap your home-made gifts prettily with ribbons, sprigs of holly or mistletoe, using a colour scheme of matching paper, ribbons and gift tags. Preserves, Brandied Mince-meat, fruits in liqueurs, pretty sweets and biscuits look most attractive arranged in baskets or boxes, or in dainty glass or china dishes. Perhaps buy a preserve pot or a pretty spoon or dish to accompany Satsuma Pine Nut Conserve. Assorted cheeses make a nice last-minute gift and look especially good placed in a basket with butter and biscuits and a pretty festive napkin. Biscuits or Gingerbread Houses make perfect novelty gifts for children. A Mini Christmas Cake with a few mince pies would make a most welcome gift for someone living alone, or make a mini-hamper of home-made goodies, such as pâté, preserves, cake, Christmas pud and biscuits.

BACON AIGRETTES

4 rashers streaky bacon, rind removed
3 teaspoons chopped fresh parsley
½ teaspoon ground black pepper
½ teaspoon Dijon mustard
vegetable oil for frying

CHOUX PASTRY: 60 g (2 oz/¼ cup) butter
75 g (2½ oz/¼ cup plus 6 teaspoons) plain flour
2 eggs

DIP: 155 ml (5 fl oz/⅔ cup) Greek yogurt
3 teaspoons chopped fresh chives
3 teaspoons mango chutney

Grill bacon until crisp; chop finely.

Mix bacon in a bowl with parsley, pepper and mustard. To make choux pastry, in a saucepan, heat 155 ml (5 fl oz/⅔ cup) water and the butter until melted. Bring to boil, remove pan from heat and immediately add all flour, beating vigorously to form a paste. Return to heat for a few seconds, stirring until paste forms a ball. Add eggs one at a time, beating until paste is very smooth and glossy. Stir in bacon mixture until well blended.

Half-fill a deep fat pan or fryer with oil. Heat to 180C (350F), or test by dropping a small piece of paste into oil: if it sizzles on contact, the oil is hot enough. Take teaspoonfuls of mixture (a little at a time) and drop into hot oil. Fry for 3-4 minutes, turning once, until puffed and golden brown. Drain on absorbent kitchen paper. Fry remaining mixture in same way. Mix together yogurt, chives and chutney. Serve with hot Bacon Aigrettes.

Makes 35-40.

— ASPARAGUS WITH CHICORY —

250 g (8 oz) asparagus spears, trimmed
3 heads of chicory
250 g (8 oz/1 cup) cream cheese
3 slices prosciutto or Parma ham

MARINADE: 1 tangerine
½ clove garlic, crushed
¼ teaspoon salt
¼ teaspoon ground black pepper
½ teaspoon Dijon mustard
2 teaspoons clear honey
4 teaspoons olive oil
2 teaspoons chopped fresh tarragon

Half-fill a shallow flameproof dish or frying
pan with water and bring to the boil. Add
asparagus and cook for 3-4 minutes until
spears are tender, then drain and cool in a
shallow dish. To make marinade, using a
zester, cut tangerine peel into fine strips,
squeeze juice from fruit and place in a bowl
with garlic, salt, pepper, mustard, honey, oil
and tarragon. Beat with a wooden spoon until
thoroughly blended. Pour over asparagus;
cover and chill for at least 1 hour.

Separate chicory leaves and cut into 2.5 cm
(1 in) lengths. Spread or pipe a little cream
cheese onto each leaf. Cut asparagus spears
into 2.5 cm (1 in) lengths and place a length
onto each chicory leaf. Cut prosciutto or ham
into thin strips and wrap a piece around each
chicory leaf. Garnish with strips of tangerine
peel, reserved from marinade.

Makes 48.

VEGETABLE CURRY ENVELOPES

60 g (2 oz) puff pastry, thawed
1 egg, beaten
1 teaspoon cumin seeds

FILLING: 15 g (½ oz/3 teaspoons) butter
1 leek, finely chopped
1 clove garlic, crushed
1 teaspoon ground cumin
1 teaspoon garam masala
2 teaspoons mango chutney
½ teaspoon finely grated lime peel
2 teaspoons lime juice
60 g (2 oz) cooked, diced potato

Melt butter for filling in a small saucepan.
Add leek and garlic to pan.

Cook quickly for 1 minute, stirring. Add
cumin, garam masala, chutney, lime peel and
juice. Stir well, cook gently for 1-2 minutes,
then add potatoes, mix well and cool.
Preheat oven to 220C (425F/Gas 7). Roll out
puff pastry very thinly to an oblong measuring
30 × 20 cm (12 × 8 in). Cut into twenty-four
5 cm (2 in) squares. Brush edges with beaten
egg and place a little filling in centre of each.

Draw all corners to centre and seal joins to
form a tiny envelope. Repeat to seal all pastry
envelopes. Arrange on a baking sheet, brush
with egg to glaze and sprinkle with cumin
seeds. Cook in the oven for 5-8 minutes until
well risen and golden brown.

Makes 24.

— OYSTERS WITH AUBERGINE —

125 g (4 oz) aubergine (eggplant), diced
salt
6 large slices white bread
60 g (2 oz/¼ cup) butter
6 teaspoons chopped fresh chives
2 teaspoons chopped fresh oregano
4 button mushrooms, finely chopped
½ teaspoon ground black pepper
2 teaspoons fromage frais
12 fresh oysters in shells
45 g (1½ oz/¾ cup) soft breadcrumbs
oregano sprigs, to garnish

Place aubergine (eggplant) in a bowl and sprinkle with salt. Leave for 30 minutes.

Preheat oven to 220C (425F/Gas 7). Cut crusts off bread and roll slices flat with a rolling pin. Cut into twenty-four 5 cm (2 in) rounds, using a daisy cutter. Spread both sides with a little butter and press into 24 bun tin shapes. Cook in the oven for 5 minutes until lightly browned. Drain and rinse aubergine (eggplant) and pat dry on absorbent kitchen paper. Melt remaining butter in a saucepan, add aubergine, chives, oregano, mushrooms and pepper and season with salt.

Fry quickly, stirring occasionally, until aubergine is tender. Stir in fromage frais. Scrub oyster shells, then open and remove oysters. Cut each in half and place ½ an oyster into each bread case. Top with aubergine (eggplant) mixture and sprinkle with breadcrumbs. Return to oven for a further 10 minutes until breadcrumbs are lightly browned. Arrange on a serving plate and garnish with oregano sprigs.

Makes 24.

OATIE BRIE CUBES

90 g (3 oz/1 ½ cups) soft breadcrumbs
30 g (1 oz/¼ cup) fine oatmeal
½ teaspoon salt
½ teaspoon ground black pepper
½ teaspoon dry mustard
2 eggs
250 g (8 oz) firm Brie or Camembert cheese
vegetable oil for frying
lime wedges, bay leaves and cranberries, to garnish

DIP: 90 g (3 oz/¾ cup) cranberries
finely grated peel and juice of 1 lime
15 g (½ oz/3 teaspoons) caster sugar

In a bowl, mix together breadcrumbs, oatmeal, salt, pepper and mustard.

Beat eggs in a small bowl. Cut cheese into bite-sized cubes, dip one cube at a time in beaten egg, then coat evenly in oatmeal mixture. Repeat to coat cheese cubes a second time in egg and oatmeal mixture. Chill until required. To make dip, place cranberries, lime peel and juice in a saucepan, bring to boil, cover and cook for 1-2 minutes until tender. Place in food processor fitted with a metal blade, add sugar and process until smooth. Place in a small serving dish.

Half-fill a deep pan or fryer with oil, heat to 180C (350F), or until a cheese cube sizzles immediately. Fry about 6 cheese cubes at a time until pale golden in colour. Drain on absorbent kitchen paper and cook remaining cheese cubes in the same way. Arrange on a serving dish with cocktail sticks. Garnish with lime wedges, bay leaves and cranberries and serve with cranberry dip.

Makes 20.

CRAB & FENNEL PUFFS

1 quantity Choux Pastry, see Bacon Aigrettes page 10
1 egg yolk
2 teaspoons sesame seeds
fennel sprigs and radish slices, to garnish

FILLING: 15 g (½ oz/3 teaspoons) butter
9 teaspoons finely chopped spring onions
9 teaspoons finely chopped fennel
90 g (3 oz) white crabmeat
60 g (2 oz) dark crabmeat
½ teaspoon finely grated lemon peel
¼ teaspoon ground black pepper
3 teaspoons thick sour cream
cayenne pepper

Preheat oven to 220C (425F/Gas 7). Grease 2 baking sheets. Make pastry, see page 10. Place mixture in a piping bag fitted with a 1 cm (½ in) plain nozzle. Pipe about 40 small rounds of mixture, spaced apart, on baking sheets. Brush with egg yolk. Sprinkle with sesame seeds. Cook in the oven for 15-20 minutes until crisp and golden brown. Cool on a wire rack. To make filling, melt butter in a small saucepan, add onions and fennel and cook for 1-2 minutes until tender.

Remove pan from heat, stir in white and dark crabmeat, lemon peel, pepper and thick sour cream until well blended. Cut each choux ball across the top and fill each with crab mixture. Dust with cayenne pepper, arrange on a serving plate and garnish with fennel sprigs and radish slices.

Makes 40.

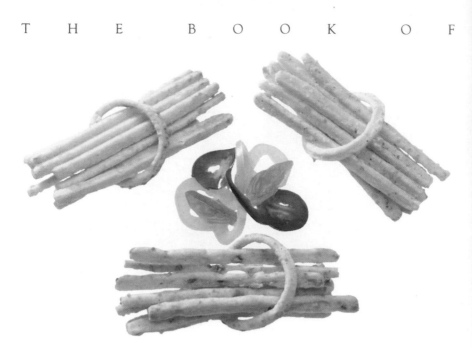

CHEESE STRAWS

250 g (8 oz/2 cups) plain flour
½ teaspoon salt
½ teaspoon cayenne pepper
½ teaspoon dry mustard
125 g (4 oz/½ cup) butter
125 g (4 oz/1 cup) grated Cheddar cheese
1 egg, beaten
4 teaspoons finely chopped red and yellow peppers
     (capsicums)
1 clove garlic, crushed
4 teaspoons chopped fresh basil and parsley
peppers (capsicums), basil and parsley, to garnish

Preheat oven to 200C (400F/Gas 6). In a
bowl, sift flour, salt, cayenne and mustard.

Cut butter into pieces, add to bowl and rub in
finely to resemble breadcrumbs. Using a fork,
stir in cheese and egg until mixture clings
together. Knead to form a smooth dough.
Cut pastry into 4 pieces. Flavour one piece
with peppers (capsicum), one with garlic and
one with herbs, kneading each piece lightly.
Roll out one piece at a time to a strip
measuring 10 cm (4 in) wide and 0.5 cm (¼
in) thick.

Using a long-bladed knife, cut into 0.5 cm
(¼ in) strips. Arrange in straight lines on
greased baking sheets. Knead each of the
flavoured trimmings together, re-roll and cut
out circles using a 5 cm (2 in) and 4.5 cm (1¾
in) plain cutter. Place on baking sheets.
Cook in the oven for 5-8 minutes until pale in
colour. Cool on wire racks. Serve straws in
bundles threaded through pastry rings,
garnished with peppers (capsicum), basil and
parsley.

Makes 100 straws plus rings.

CRISPY PESTO PRAWNS

12 Mediterranean (king) prawns, peeled
6 large slices white bread
60 g (2 oz/¼ cup) butter
1 clove garlic, crushed
4 teaspoons pesto sauce
1 teaspoon finely grated lemon peel
¼ teaspoon salt
¼ teaspoon ground black pepper
lemon triangles, basil leaves or parsley sprigs, to garnish

Cut each prawn in ½ across width. Cut crusts off bread and, using a rolling pin, roll each slice flat.

Place butter in a small bowl, beat until soft and smooth. Stir in garlic, pesto sauce, lemon peel and salt and pepper. Beat together until smooth and well blended. Spread both sides of each slice of bread with butter mixture, then cut each slice into 4 triangles.

Place a prawn in centre of each bread triangle, fold 2 side points to centre and secure with a cocktail stick. Arrange on a grid in a grill pan and cook under a moderately hot grill until bread is lightly browned. Serve hot, garnished with lemon triangles, basil leaves or parsley sprigs.

Makes 24.

FESTIVE DIP SELECTION

1 small aubergine (eggplant)
2 cloves garlic
125 ml (4 fl oz/½ cup) thick sour cream
salt and ground black pepper
3 teaspoons chopped fresh rosemary
250 g (8 oz/1 cup) cream cheese
6 teaspoons fromage frais
30 g (1 oz/¼ cup) chopped fresh mixed herbs (parsley, basil, thyme, oregano and chervil)
125 g (4 oz/⅔ cup) red lentils, cooked in 470 ml (15 fl oz/1¾ cups) water
155 ml (5 fl oz/⅔ cup) Greek yogurt
mixed vegetable sticks such as courgettes (zucchini), peppers (capsicums), celery, cucumber and carrots; baby sweetcorn, cherry tomatoes and radishes, to serve

Preheat oven to 220C (425F/Gas 7), or use a hot grill. Bake or grill aubergine (eggplant) until skin has charred and flesh is tender, turning once. Cut aubergine (eggplant) in half, scoop out flesh; cool. Using a food processor fitted with a metal blade, add aubergine (eggplant), 1 clove garlic, thick sour cream, salt and pepper to taste and rosemary; process until mixture is smooth and creamy. Place in a serving bowl. Place cream cheese, fromage frais, mixed herbs and salt and pepper in a bowl and beat until soft and well blended. Spoon into a serving dish.

Cool lentils. In a food processor, place remaining garlic, salt and pepper to taste, lentils and yogurt and process until creamy and smooth. Place in a serving bowl. Serve dips accompanied by mixed vegetable sticks, baby sweetcorn, cherry tomatoes and radishes.

Each dip serves 6-8.

CURRY WHIRLS

155 g (5 oz/1¼ cups) plain flour
1 teaspoon curry powder
½ teaspoon salt
½ teaspoon pepper
½ teaspoon dry mustard
125 g (4 oz/½ cup) butter
6 teaspoons grated Parmesan cheese
a little beaten egg
1 teaspoon coriander seeds

Preheat oven to 220C (425F/Gas 7). Sift flour, curry powder, salt, pepper and mustard into a bowl. Cut the butter into pieces, add to bowl and rub in finely to resemble breadcrumbs.

Using a fork, stir in Parmesan cheese and egg until mixture clings together. Mix to form a soft dough. Place mixture in a nylon piping bag fitted with a star nozzle. Pipe 40 swirls of mixture onto lightly greased baking sheets, spacing them apart.

Sprinkle each swirl with coriander seeds and cook in the oven for 10-15 minutes until lightly browned at edges. Cool on a wire rack. Arrange on a plate to serve.

Makes 40.

PEPPER-FILLED LEAVES

10 small spinach leaves
10 small lettuce leaves
10 small radicchio leaves

FILLING: 30 g (1 oz/2 tablespoons) long-grain rice
5 rashers streaky bacon
4 teaspoons chopped pickled vegetables
60 g (2 oz/¼ cup) curd cheese
1 teaspoon Dijon mustard
½ teaspoon salt
½ teaspoon ground black pepper
1 small red pepper (capsicum), seeded
1 small yellow pepper (capsicum), seeded

Bring a saucepan of water to the boil. Add spinach leaves, bring back to boil; remove leaves quickly and refresh leaves in cold water. Drain thoroughly and pat dry on absorbent kitchen paper. Repeat this process with remaining leaves. To make filling, cook rice in boiling salted water until tender; drain and cool. Grill bacon until crisp, then chop bacon and pickled vegetables finely. Place curd cheese in a bowl and beat until smooth. Add rice, bacon, pickled vegetables, mustard and salt and pepper; stir until well blended.

Spread leaves out flat on a board, place a teaspoonful of mixture on each. Roll up neatly and secure each with a cocktail stick. Cut peppers (capsicums) into thin rings, then cut rings into 4 and use to garnish filled leaves. Arrange on a serving plate and serve with a spicy sauce, if desired.

Makes 30.

FETA CHEESE KEBABS

220 g (7 oz) feta cheese
¼ red pepper (capsicum)
¼ yellow pepper (capsicum)
1 courgette (zucchini)
¼ aubergine (eggplant)
thyme sprigs, to garnish

MARINADE: 6 teaspoons olive oil
3 teaspoons raspberry vinegar
1 teaspoon pink peppercorns, crushed
1 teaspoon clear honey
½ teaspoon Dijon mustard
2 teaspoons chopped fresh thyme
¼ teaspoon salt
½ teaspoon ground black pepper

To make marinade, place oil, vinegar, peppercorns, honey, mustard, thyme, salt and pepper in a large bowl. Stir mixture together with a wooden spoon until thoroughly blended. Cut feta cheese, peppers (capsicums), courgette (zucchini) and aubergine (eggplant) into bite-sized pieces. Add to marinade, stir well to coat evenly, cover with plastic wrap and leave in a cool place for at least 1 hour.

Thread one piece of each ingredient onto wooden cocktail sticks. Just before serving, cook under a hot grill for 2-3 minutes until vegetables are just tender. Arrange on a serving plate, garnished with sprigs of thyme.

Makes 24.

— CHICKEN LIVER POUCHES —

2 leaves filo or strudel pastry, thawed
60 g (2 oz/¼ cup) butter, melted
1 teaspoon poppy seeds
oregano sprigs and tomato, to garnish

FILLING: 15 g (½ oz/3 teaspoons) butter
1 clove garlic, crushed
125 g (4 oz) chicken livers, chopped
3 teaspoons chopped fresh oregano
¼ teaspoon salt
¼ teaspoon ground black pepper
2 teaspoons plain flour
2 teaspoons Marsala
6 teaspoons single (light) cream

Preheat oven to 200C (400F/Gas 6). To make filling, melt butter in a small saucepan, add garlic and chicken livers and fry quickly for 30 seconds. Stir in oregano, salt, pepper and flour until well blended. Add Marsala and cream, bring to boil, stirring, then remove from heat and cool. Brush filo pastry sheets with melted butter, place one on top of the other. Using a sharp knife, cut into twenty-four 6 cm (2½ in) squares. Spoon a little filling onto each square.

Draw up corners of the pastry and press firmly together. Press down slightly to flatten. Brush each pouch with remaining melted butter, sprinkle with poppy seeds and cook in the oven for 5 minutes until golden brown. Arrange on a warm serving dish, garnished with oregano and tomato.

Makes 24.

COCKTAIL BISCUITS

375 g (12 oz/3 cups) plain flour
1/2 teaspoon salt
1/2 teaspoon cayenne pepper
1 teaspoon dry mustard
185 g (6 oz/3/4 cup) butter, diced
125 g (4 oz/1 cup) grated Cheddar cheese
1 egg, beaten

FLAVOURINGS: 1 teaspoon sesame seeds
1 teaspoon poppy seeds
1 teaspoon curry paste
2 teaspoons tomato purée

In a bowl, sift flour, salt, cayenne and mustard. Add butter and rub in finely.

Using a fork, stir in cheese and egg until mixture clings together. Knead to form a smooth dough. Cut pastry into 4 pieces. Knead sesame seeds into one piece and poppy seeds into another. Form both into 15 cm (6 in) rolls. Wrap separately in plastic wrap. Roll remaining 2 pieces of pastry into 20 × 15 cm (8 × 6 in) rectangles. Spread one piece with curry paste and the other with tomato purée. Roll up each from a long edge to form 2 firm rolls. Wrap in plastic wrap. Chill all the rolls until firm, or freeze until required.

Preheat oven to 200C (400F/Gas 6). Line several baking sheets with non-stick baking paper. Cut each roll into thin slices and arrange a little apart on baking sheets lined with baking parchment. Bake for 6-8 minutes until pale in colour. Cool, then transfer to wire racks.

Makes 96.

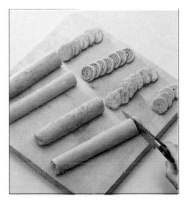

LAMB & WALNUT BITES

250 g (8 oz) lamb fillet
60 g (2 oz/1 cup) soft breadcrumbs
1 shallot
2 teaspoons fresh rosemary
1 teaspoon salt
½ teaspoon ground black pepper
1 egg
5 pickled walnuts
plain flour
1 onion, finely chopped
1 clove garlic, crushed
3 large tomatoes, peeled, seeded and chopped
3 teaspoons chopped fresh basil
vegetable oil for frying
rosemary or parsley sprigs and cherry tomatoes, to garnish

Put lamb in a food processor fitted with a metal blade and process until finely chopped. Add breadcrumbs, shallot, rosemary, salt, pepper and egg. Process again until smooth. Cut pickled walnuts into small pieces. Take a teaspoonful of meat mixture, press into a flat round using a little flour to prevent sticking, and place a piece of walnut in centre and form into a neat ball. Repeat to make 35-40 balls in total.

Put onion, garlic and tomatoes in a small saucepan and cook rapidly, stirring occasionally, until mixture is thick. Stir in basil and place in a serving dish. Half-fill a small pan with oil and heat to 180C (350F), or until a meatball placed in the oil sizzles immediately. Fry meatballs, in several batches, for 2-3 minutes until lightly browned. Drain on absorbent kitchen paper. Arrange on a serving plate and garnish. Serve with the sauce.

Makes 35-40.

CHEESE THINS

125 g (4 oz/1 cup) plain flour
½ teaspoon salt
½ teaspoon pepper
½ teaspoon dry mustard
125 g (4 oz/½ cup) butter
125 g (4 oz/1 cup) grated Cheddar cheese
4 teaspoons fine oatmeal
1 teaspoon cayenne pepper
1 egg white

Preheat oven to 220C (425F/Gas 7). Lightly butter 2 baking sheets. Sift flour, salt, pepper and mustard into a bowl. Cut butter into pieces, add to bowl and rub in finely until mixture begins to cling together.

Using a fork, stir in cheese and mix to a soft dough. Knead on a lightly floured surface and roll out very thinly. Using a 2.5 cm (1 in) oval cutter, cut out 80 oval shapes. Arrange on baking sheets, spaced apart.

Mix together oatmeal and cayenne. Brush each oval with egg white and sprinkle with oatmeal mixture. Bake in the oven for 5-6 minutes until pale in colour. Cool on baking sheets, then remove carefully with a palette knife.

Makes 80.

— HERBED CRÊPE PINWHEELS —

60 g (2 oz/½ cup) plain flour
¼ teaspoon salt
¼ teaspoon ground black pepper
1 egg
125 ml (4 fl oz/¼ cup) milk
3 teaspoons chopped fresh basil
vegetable oil for frying
cherry tomato wedges and herb sprigs, to garnish

FILLING: 8 large spinach leaves
125 g (4 oz/½ cup) soft cheese with herbs and garlic
8 thin slices prosciutto or Parma ham

Sift flour, salt and pepper into a bowl. Add egg and half the milk; beat until smooth.

Stir in remaining milk and basil and beat until well blended. Heat a little oil in a small frying pan, add a spoonful of batter and swirl pan to coat thinly. Cook until crêpe is pale golden on both sides, turning once. Place on absorbent kitchen paper. Repeat to make 8 crêpes in total.

To make filling, cook spinach leaves for 1 minute in boiling salted water; drain and cool. Take one crêpe at a time and cover with a spinach leaf, then spread with a little cheese and cover with a slice of prosciutto or Parma ham. Roll up firmly and wrap in plastic wrap. Repeat with remaining ingredients to make 8 crêpe rolls. Just before serving, cut each roll into 1 cm (½ in) slices. Arrange on a serving plate and garnish with tomato wedges and sprigs of herbs.

Makes 48.

PARTY QUICHES

PASTRY: 60 g (2 oz/½ cup) plain flour
¼ teaspoon salt
30 g (1 oz/6 teaspoons) butter

FILLING: 1 egg
6 teaspoons single (light) cream
¼ teaspoon salt
¼ teaspoon pepper
¼ teaspoon dry mustard
2 teaspoons each finely chopped peppers (capsicums),
  chopped button mushrooms, crisp crumbled bacon
  and fresh herbs

Sift flour and salt into a bowl. Cut the butter into small pieces.

Add butter to bowl and rub in finely until mixture resembles breadcrumbs. Using a fork, stir in 2-3 teaspoons water until mixture begins to bind together. Knead to form a firm dough. Roll out pastry thinly on a lightly floured surface and use to line 24 tiny pastry boat moulds or tiny round tartlet tins. Prick bases and chill for 1 hour. Preheat oven to 220C (425F/Gas 7). Bake pastry moulds for 5 minutes, then remove from oven.

To make filling, put egg, cream, salt, pepper and mustard in a bowl. Whisk until well blended. Half-fill each pastry case with egg mixture, then fill 6 with chopped peppers (capsicums), 6 with mushrooms, 6 with bacon and the remainder with herbs. Return to the oven for a further 5-6 minutes until filling has set. Cool slightly, then slip pastry cases out of moulds. Serve warm or cold.

Makes 24.

MUSSELS WITH BASIL

12 fresh mussels
30 g (1 oz/6 teaspoons) butter
2 tomatoes, skinned, seeded and chopped
6 teaspoons chopped chives
6 teaspoons chopped fresh basil
1 clove garlic, crushed
3 teaspoons tomato purée
¼ teaspoon salt
¼ teaspoon ground black pepper
½ teaspoon caster sugar
6 slices brown bread
6 teaspoons vegetable oil
3 prunes, stoned and chopped, and basil leaves, to
  garnish

Scrub mussels, remove beards and place in a saucepan. Cover with a lid and heat gently until shells have opened. Cool. Melt butter in a saucepan, add tomatoes, chives, basil, garlic, tomato purée, salt, pepper and sugar. Bring to boil, stirring occasionally and cook gently for 2 minutes until thick.

Cut bread into 24 daisy shapes using a 2.5 cm (1 in) daisy cutter. Heat oil in a frying pan and fry bread shapes until golden brown; drain on kitchen paper. Remove mussels from shells, cut each in ½ and place on bread shapes. Top each with a spoonful of tomato filling and garnish with pieces of prune and basil leaves.

Makes 24.

–CREAMY-FILLED QUAILS' EGGS–

12 quails' eggs
4 large slices brown toast
15 g (½ oz/3 teaspoons) butter
2 teaspoons red lumpfish caviar and chervil sprigs, to
  garnish

FILLING: 60 g (2 oz) chick-peas, cooked
6 teaspoons double (thick) cream
½ teaspoon salt
½ teaspoon ground black pepper
1 teaspoon Dijon mustard

Bring a small saucepan of water to the boil,
add quails' eggs and cook for 3 minutes.

Drain and cover with cold water, then shell
and cut eggs into halves. Scoop out yolks. To
make filling, place chick-peas in a food
processor fitted with a metal blade. Process
until smooth. Add cream, salt, pepper,
mustard and egg yolks and process until
smooth and creamy. Place chick-pea filling in
a piping bag fitted with a small star nozzle.
Pipe swirls of mixture onto egg whites.

Cut toast into ovals or rounds, using a 2.5 cm
(1 in) cutter. Spread thinly with butter and
place a filled egg on each one. Garnish with a
little lumpfish caviar and chervil sprigs.

Makes 24.

— CRISPY BACON PINWHEELS —

90 g (3 oz/³⁄₄ cup) grated Cheddar cheese
¹⁄₄ teaspoon salt
¹⁄₄ teaspoon pepper
¹⁄₂ teaspoon Dijon mustard
6 teaspoons Greek yogurt
6 large slices white bread
45 g (1¹⁄₂ oz/9 teaspoons) butter
6 rashers streaky bacon
celery leaves and radish leaves, to garnish

In a bowl, mix together cheese, salt, pepper, mustard and yogurt. Cut crusts off bread and roll slices flat with a rolling pin.

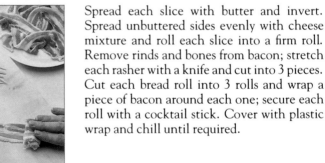

Spread each slice with butter and invert. Spread unbuttered sides evenly with cheese mixture and roll each slice into a firm roll. Remove rinds and bones from bacon; stretch each rasher with a knife and cut into 3 pieces. Cut each bread roll into 3 rolls and wrap a piece of bacon around each one; secure each roll with a cocktail stick. Cover with plastic wrap and chill until required.

Just before serving, remove plastic wrap and grill bacon-wrapped rolls under a hot grill until bacon is crisp and golden brown. Cool slightly, remove cocktail sticks and then cut each roll into 3 slices. Arrange on a serving plate and garnish with celery leaves and radish slices.

Makes 54.

— MUSHROOMS & GRAPEFRUIT —

250 g (8 oz) button mushrooms
fresh mint leaves or chives, to garnish

MARINADE: 1 large pink grapefruit
90 ml (3 fl oz/⅓ cup) ginger wine
2 teaspoons mint jelly
½ teaspoon salt
½ teaspoon ground black pepper
1 teaspoon Dijon mustard

To make marinade, cut away grapefruit peel and white pith from flesh, allowing juice to fall into a small saucepan. Cut out segments between membranes and place on a plate.

Squeeze remaining juice from membranes into saucepan. Add ginger wine, mint jelly, salt, pepper and mustard; bring to the boil and stir in mushrooms. Pour into a bowl and leave until cold.

Cut grapefruit segments into bite-sized pieces. Thread 2 mushrooms and a piece of grapefruit onto each cocktail stick and garnish with mint leaves or chives.

Makes 24.

— AVOCADO SALMON ROLLS —

90 g (3 oz) sliced smoked salmon
3 slices rye bread
30 g (1 oz/3 teaspoons) butter
dill sprigs and lemon twists, to garnish

FILLING: **60 g (2 oz/¼ cup) full fat soft cheese**
½ avocado, mashed
2 teaspoons chopped fresh dill
1 small tomato, skinned, seeded and chopped
¼ teaspoon ground black pepper

To make filling, put cheese in a bowl and beat until soft. Add avocado and stir until blended.

Add dill, chopped tomato and pepper and stir gently. Place in a piping bag fitted with 1 cm (½ in) plain nozzle. Cut smoked salmon into 20 oblongs measuring about 4 × 2.5 cm (1½ × 1 in). Pipe a length of cheese mixture across top of a short edge of each salmon oblong. Roll up each one neatly.

Spread rye bread with butter, then cut into 20 rectangles to fit salmon rolls. Place a salmon roll on each piece and garnish with sprigs of dill and lemon twists.

Makes 20.

— FILLED BUTTON RAREBITS —

60 g (2 oz/1 cup) soft white breadcrumbs
60 g (2 oz/¼ cup) chopped ham
3 teaspoons chopped fresh parsley
3 teaspoons fromage frais
24 button mushrooms
4 large slices white bread
30 g (1 oz/6 teaspoons) soft tub margarine
3 teaspoons cider
90 g (3 oz/¾ cup) grated Cheddar cheese
1 teaspoon Worcestershire sauce
¼ teaspoon salt
¼ teaspoon ground black pepper
¼ teaspoon dry mustard
fresh herbs, to garnish

Preheat oven to 220C (425F/Gas 7). In a bowl, mix together breadcrumbs, ham, parsley and fromage frais. Remove stalks from mushrooms, chop finely and add to bowl; stir thoroughly. Press this mixture into centre of each mushroom. Cut out rounds of bread to match size of mushrooms, using a plain cutter. Spread both sides with margarine and sit a mushroom on top of each bread round. Arrange on a baking sheet and cook in the oven for 5 minutes, then remove and keep on one side.

Place cider in a saucepan and bring to the boil. Remove pan from heat, stir in cheese, Worcestershire sauce, salt, pepper and mustard; beat well together. Spoon a little cheese mixture over top of each filled mushroom. Return to oven and cook for a further 3-4 minutes until cheese has melted and browned slightly. Arrange on a serving dish and garnish with fresh herbs.

Makes 24.

FONDANT SWEETS

250 g (8 oz) ready-to-roll fondant icing
pink, green, yellow, mauve and orange food colourings

FLAVOURINGS: 3 marrons glacés
3 pieces crystallised ginger
a few drops of peppermint oil
1 teaspoon each of finely grated orange, lemon and lime
  peel

Cut fondant icing into 6 pieces. Keep one piece plain and, using food colourings, tint remaining 5 pieces a very pale pink, green, yellow, mauve and orange.

Cut 2 marrons glacés and pink fondant into 8 pieces, wrap each piece of marrons glacés in pink fondant and shape into a neat ball. Repeat with mauve fondant and 2 pieces of crystallised ginger to make oval-shaped sweets. Decorate tops with remaining marrons glacés and ginger.

Flavour white fondant with peppermint oil and roll out to 0.5 cm (¼ in) thickness. Using a small round or crescent-shaped cutter, cut out 8-10 shapes. Knead orange peel into orange fondant, lemon peel into yellow fondant and lime peel into green fondant. Shape each piece into tiny pinwheels, squares, diamonds or trefoil shapes. Or press small pieces of fondant into plastic sweet moulds. Dry out completely on a paper-lined baking sheet.

Makes 40.

— HAND-MADE CHOCOLATES —

90 g (3 oz) ready-to-roll fondant icing
rose and violet flavourings
pink and mauve food colourings
60 g (2 oz) white marzipan
6 maraschino cherries
6 crème de menthe cherries
6 Brazil nuts
6 whole almonds
185 g (6 oz) plain (dark) chocolate
185 g (6 oz) white chocolate
185 g (6 oz) milk chocolate
crystallised rose and violet petals

Cut fondant into 2 pieces: flavour ½ with rose flavouring and colour pale pink.

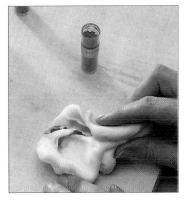

Flavour remaining piece with violet flavouring and colour pale mauve. Roll out fondant to 1 cm (½ in) thickness and cut into shapes using cocktail cutters. Place on a non-stick paper-lined baking sheet. Shape marzipan into various shapes by rolling bite-sized pieces between hands into balls, logs or ovals. Arrange on baking sheet. Leave to dry for several hours or overnight. Pat cherries dry. Toast nuts until golden brown.

Melt each type of chocolate in separate bowls over hand-hot water and stir until melted. Using a fork, dip one prepared centre at a time into chocolate; tap to remove excess, and place chocolate on a paper-lined baking sheet. Leave plain, or mark top with a fork or with piped chocolate. Decorate rose and violet centres with crystallised petals. Continue to dip all centres, giving a variety of white, plain (dark), or milk chocolate.

Makes about 30.

— CHOCOLATE TRUFFLE CUPS —

500 g (1 lb) white chocolate
60 g (2 oz/¼ cup) unsalted butter, softened
6 teaspoons whipping cream
4 teaspoons cherry brandy
pink, green and yellow food colourings
4 teaspoons Chartreuse
4 teaspoons apricot brandy
6 pistachio nuts, chopped

Break up chocolate and place in a dry bowl over a saucepan of hand-hot water. Stir occasionally until melted; remove bowl from pan and cool. Place 36 foil cases on a tray, spoon a little chocolate into each one.

Using a fine brush, coat inside of each case; leave to set. Add soft butter and cream to remaining chocolate; stir until smooth. Divide mixture between 3 bowls. Flavour one with cherry brandy and tint pink; flavour another with Chartreuse and tint green, and the other with apricot brandy and tint with yellow and pink colouring to give an apricot colour.

When chocolate mixtures are set enough to peak softly, place each in a separate piping bag fitted with a small star nozzle; pipe swirls of each flavour into 12 chocolate cases. Sprinkle with pistachio nuts and leave to set. Pack in pretty containers.

Makes 36.

KUMQUATS IN COGNAC

500 g (1 lb) kumquats
375 g (12 oz/1½ cups) granulated sugar
155 ml (5 fl oz/⅔ cup) cognac

Have ready 2 or 3 small, clean, dry, warm sterilised glass jars with well-fitting lids. Remove stalks and wash kumquats thoroughly; dry on absorbent kitchen paper. Place 315 ml (10 fl oz/1¼ cups) water in a medium-sized saucepan, add 125 g (4 oz/½ cup) sugar and heat gently, stirring occasionally, until sugar has dissolved.

Bring to boil, add kumquats and cook very gently for 2-3 minutes, taking care kumquats do not split open. Remove kumquats with a slotted spoon and place on a plate. Reserve syrup. Place kumquats carefully in jars without packing them too tightly, so they come to neck of jar. Measure 155 ml (5 fl oz/⅔ cup) of remaining syrup and put in a saucepan with remaining sugar. Stir over a gentle heat until sugar has dissolved.

Boil rapidly for 1 minute until syrupy. Test by placing a drop of syrup between 2 cold teaspoons: press together, then pull apart – a fine thread of sugar should form. Pour sugar syrup into measuring jug and add the same amount of cognac. Stir well and fill each jar to the brim with cognac syrup. Seal jars with well-fitting lids, label and store in a cool place for up to 3 months.

Makes 2-3 jars.

SPICED CITRUS SLICES

3 thin-skinned oranges
4 thin-skinned lemons
5 limes
625 ml (20 fl oz/2½ cups) white wine vinegar
1.25 kg (2½ lb/4½ cups) granulated sugar
2 cinnamon sticks
7g (¼ oz/2 teaspoons) whole cloves
6 blades of mace

Scrub fruit thoroughly, then cut into 0.3 cm (⅛ in) thick slices. Lay slices in a stainless steel or enamel saucepan and just cover with water. Bring to boil, then cover and cook very gently for about 15 minutes until peel is tender. Drain slices and reserve liquor.

In another saucepan, gently heat vinegar, sugar and spices, stirring occasionally, until sugar has dissolved. Bring to boil, then add fruit slices. Add reserved liquor to cover fruit if necessary, then cook very gently for 15 minutes until peel looks transparent.

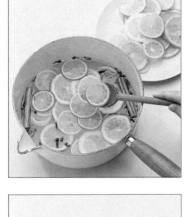

Arrange fruit slices in small, clean, hot jars, alternating slices, or packing each separately, as desired. Bring syrup to the boil, discard cinnamon and immediately fill each jar to top. Cover with airtight, vinegar-proof lids. When cold, label and store in a cool place for up to 6 months.

Makes 4 small jars.

FRUITS IN CHARTREUSE

10 fresh lychees or 470 g (15 oz) can lychees
250 g (8 oz/2 cups) cherries or 470 g (15 oz) can
  cherries
250 g (8 oz/1 cup) granulated sugar
315 ml (10 fl oz/1 ¼ cups) Chartreuse or Benedectine
  liqueur

Peel fresh lychees and carefully remove stones, keeping fruit whole, or drain and stone canned lychees. Remove stalks and wash fresh cherries, or drain canned cherries, and dry on absorbent kitchen paper. Pierce skins of cherries all over with a clean needle or fine skewer.

Have ready 3 or 4 very small, clean, dry, sterilised jars with well-fitting lids. Arrange a layer of cherries in one clean jar and sprinkle with about 1 tablespoon sugar. Arrange a layer of lychees on top and sprinkle with more sugar. Continue to layer cherries, sugar and lychees until jar is loosely filled to neck of jar, do not pack fruit in tightly. Sprinkle with a final layer of sugar.

Fill jar to the top with Chartreuse or Benedictine and seal with a clean lid. Repeat to fill remaining small jars with fruits, sugar and liqueur. Store in a cool, dry place for up to 6 months. Gift wrap for presents.

Makes 3 or 4 small jars.

SATSUMA PINE NUT CONSERVE

1 kg (2 lb) satsumas
1 kg (2 lb/4 cups) granulated sugar
60 ml (2 fl oz/¼ cup) orange flower water
60 g (2 oz/½ cup) pine nuts

Scrub satsumas well, then using a potato peeler or sharp knife, pare peel from satsumas, not including white pith. Cut peel into fine strips and place in a large saucepan with 155 ml (5 fl oz/⅔ cup) water. Bring to boil, cover and cook gently for 1 hour, or until tender.

Cut satsumas in half, squeeze juice into a jug and make up to 470 ml (15 fl oz/1¾ cups) with water, if necessary. Reserve all pips, place in a piece of muslin and tie securely with string. Place in a saucepan with satsuma shells and 470 ml (15 fl oz/1¾ cups) water. Bring to boil, cover and simmer for 1 hour. Strain liquid into saucepan containing strips of peel. Stir in sugar and juice and bring to boil, stirring, until sugar has dissolved.

Boil rapidly for 5-10 minutes until setting point is reached. To test, spoon a little conserve onto a cold plate, leave for a few minutes, then push with your finger: if surface wrinkles, setting point has been reached. Add orange flower water and pine nuts, bring to boil and boil for 2 minutes. Cool for 30 minutes, stir, then pour into warm, dry, sterilised pots. Cover with wax discs; seal. Store in a cool, dry place.

Makes 1.5 kg (3 lb).

— BRANDIED MINCEMEAT —

500 g (1 lb/3 cups) raisins
500 g (1 lb/3 cups) sultanas
500 g (1 lb/3⅓ cups) currants
125 g (4 oz/1 cup) dried apricots
125 g (4 oz/¾ cup) stoned dates
185 g (6 oz/1 cup) candied peel
125 g (4 oz/¼ cup) whole almonds
500 g (1 lb) cooking apples, peeled and cored
finely grated peel and juice of 2 lemons
375 g (12 oz/2¼ cups) light soft brown sugar
250 g (8 oz/1 cup) unsalted butter, melted
3 teaspoons ground mixed spice
155 ml (5 fl oz/⅔ cup) brandy

In a bowl, put raisins, sultanas and currants.

Chop or mince apricots, dates, candied peel, almonds and apples. Add to bowl with lemon peel and juice and mix well together. Stir in sugar, butter, mixed spice and brandy. Stir the mixture until evenly blended, cover bowl with plastic wrap and leave in a cool place for 2 days.

Preheat the oven to 200C (400F/Gas 6). Thoroughly wash and dry six 500 g (1 lb) jam jars, stand them on a paper-lined baking sheet and place in the oven until hot. Stir mincemeat thoroughly, then spoon into hot jars, filling each to the top. Place a wax disc on top of each and cellophane covers over the jars, securing each with an elastic band. Label clearly and store in a cool, dry place for up to 6 months.

Makes 3 kg (6 lb).

— ROAST STUFFED TURKEY —

4 kg (8 lb) oven-ready turkey with giblets
250 g (8 oz/4¼ cups) soft white breadcrumbs
1 large onion, finely chopped
3 sticks celery, finely chopped
finely grated peel and juice of 1 lemon
8 plums, chopped
155 ml (5 fl oz/⅔ cup) red wine
500 g (1 lb/2 cups) chestnut purée
3 teaspoons each of chopped fresh sage, thyme and
    oregano
salt and pepper
500 g (1 lb) rashers fat streaky bacon
60 g (2 oz/½ cup) plain flour

Remove giblets from turkey, place in a saucepan with 625 ml (20 fl oz/2½ cups) water and bring to boil. Cover and simmer for 1 hour. Strain stock into a bowl; reserve liver. In a saucepan, place breadcrumbs, onion, celery, lemon peel and juice, plums and wine. Bring to boil, stirring, and cook for 1 minute. Put chestnut purée, herbs, salt and pepper to taste and turkey liver into a food processor fitted with a metal blade. Process until smooth. Add breadcrumb mixture and process until evenly blended.

Place ⅓ stuffing into neck end of turkey, pull over flap of skin and secure under turkey with skewers or string. Fill cavity of turkey with remaining stuffing, pull skin over parson's nose and secure with skewers or string. Truss turkey with string, securing wings and legs closely to body, and place in a roasting tin.

Cover the whole turkey with rashers of streaky bacon to help keep it moist during cooking.

Preheat oven to 190C (375F/Gas 5). Cook turkey in the oven for 2 hours, remove from oven; remove bacon if you require it for serving, and cover turkey and tin with thick foil. Return to oven for a further 1-1½ hours until turkey is tender and only clear juices run when pierced with a sharp pointed knife between legs of turkey. Leave to stand in tin for 20 minutes before removing. Remove any skewers or trussing string and place turkey on a warmed serving dish. Chop crispy bacon finely and serve with turkey.

To make gravy, blend flour and a little stock together in a pan until smooth. Pour remaining stock into roasting tin, stir well, strain gravy into saucepan with flour mixture. Bring to boil, stirring until thickened; cook for 2 minutes. Season to taste with salt and pepper and pour into a gravy boat. Serve turkey with bread sauce, chipolata sausages, crisp bacon and gravy.

Serves 10.

— APPLE & WALNUT STUFFING —

30 g (1 oz/6 teaspoons) butter
4 shallots, chopped
500 g (1 lb) cooking apples, grated
finely grated peel and juice of 1 lemon
125 g (4 oz/2 cups) soft white breadcrumbs
6 teaspoons chopped fresh thyme
½ teaspoon salt
½ teaspoon ground black pepper
60 g (2 oz/½ cup) chopped walnuts
5 pickled walnuts, sliced
1 egg, beaten

Melt butter in a saucepan, add shallots, apples, lemon peel and juice.

Cook over a moderate heat, stirring occasionally, until onion and apple are tender. Remove saucepan from heat. In a bowl, mix together breadcrumbs, thyme, salt, pepper and chopped and pickled walnuts.

Add apple mixture and beaten egg and stir well until evenly blended.

Sufficient for a 2.5-3 kg (5-6 lb) goose or duck. Double the quantities for a large turkey.

CRANBERRY ORANGE STUFFING

250 g (8 oz/2 cups) cranberries
finely grated peel and juice of 2 oranges
9 teaspoons clear honey
30 g (1 oz/6 teaspoons) butter
2 onions, chopped
1 teaspoon salt
½ teaspoon ground black pepper
½ teaspoon cayenne pepper
1 teaspoon ground mace
4 teaspoons chopped fresh sage
250 g (8 oz/4¼ cups) soft white breadcrumbs
90 g (6 oz/½ cup) pine nuts

Place cranberries, orange peel and juice in a saucepan.

Bring to boil, cover and simmer very gently for 1 minute until just tender. Remove saucepan from heat. Stir in honey and pour cranberries into a bowl. Melt butter in a saucepan, stir in onions and cook gently for 2 minutes until tender. Add salt, pepper, cayenne, mace and sage; mix until well blended.

Stir onion mixture into cranberries with breadcrumbs and pine nuts until well mixed.

Sufficient for a 4 kg (8 lb) turkey or a large goose. Halve the quantity for a duck.

GOOSEBERRY GOOSE

4 kg (8 lb) oven-ready goose, with giblets
12 rashers streaky bacon
3 teaspoons Dijon mustard
250 ml (8 fl oz/1 cup) elderflower wine
500 g (1 lb) gooseberries, cooked
3 teaspoons arrowroot
30 g (1 oz/5 teaspoons) caster sugar
50 g (2 oz) elderberries, if desired

STUFFING: 30 g (1 oz/6 teaspoons) butter
6 shallots, finely chopped
155 ml (5 fl oz/²⁄₃ cup) gooseberry juice
30 g (1 oz/1¼ cups) chopped fresh mixed herbs
375 g (12 oz/6¼ cups) soft breadcrumbs
1 teaspoon salt
1 teaspoon ground black pepper

Preheat oven to 220C (425F/Gas 7). Remove giblets from goose; reserve liver. Use giblets to make stock. Prick goose skin all over. To make stuffing, melt butter in a pan, add shallots and liver; fry for 2 minutes. Stir in ½ gooseberry juice, herbs, all but 6 teaspoons of breadcrumbs and salt and pepper. Stuff neck end of goose; place remainder in body cavity. Cover goose with bacon; cook in oven for 45 minutes. Reduce oven to 190C (375F/Gas 5); cook for 1½ hours, pouring off excess fat during cooking.

Remove bacon, chop very finely; mix with remaining breadcrumbs. Brush goose with mustard; sprinkle with crumb mixture. Return to oven for a further 20-30 minutes until meat is tender. Place on a serving plate. Pour away excess fat, add 60 ml (2 fl oz/¼ cup) stock to roasting tin, mix with remaining gooseberry juice, add wine, gooseberries, arrowroot and sugar. Boil for 1 minute, stirring. Process until smooth. Strain sauce and stir in elderberries, if desired.

Serves 6-8.

SPICED HONEY GAMMON

1.5 kg (3 lb) joint wood-smoked gammon
finely shredded peel and juice of 2 oranges
6 teaspoons clear honey
1 teaspoon ground mace
1 teaspoon grated fresh root ginger
125 g (4 oz) kumquats, sliced
6 teaspoons whole cloves
3 teaspoons cornflour

Soak gammon joint overnight in a bowl of cold water. Drain, transfer to a large saucepan and cover with fresh cold water. Bring to boil, cover and cook for 30 minutes. Drain and cool. Remove skin from gammon, leaving a layer of fat on surface of gammon.

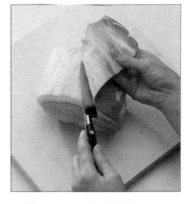

Score fat on the surface of gammon into a lattice pattern with a sharp knife. Preheat oven to 190C (375F/Gas 5); place gammon in roasting tin. In a bowl, mix together orange peel, juice, honey, mace and ginger until evenly blended. Brush a little mixture over surface of gammon and bake in the oven for 30 minutes. Remove gammon from oven, brush surface with more orange mixture. Cover surface of gammon with kumquat slices, held in position with whole cloves.

Return to oven for a further 30-40 minutes until gammon is golden brown and tender. Remove and place on a serving dish. Keep warm. Add 185 ml (6 fl oz/¾ cup) water to roasting tin, stir to mix juices, then strain into a saucepan. Blend cornflour with remaining orange juice and honey mixture, add to pan, bring to boil and cook for 1 minute. Pour into a jug and serve with gammon. Garnish with remaining kumquat slices.

Serves 8.

BOXING DAY TERRINE

500 g (1 lb) belly pork, boned
500 g (1 lb) unsmoked streaky bacon
500 g (1 lb) chicken breast fillets
500 g (1 lb) pie veal
155 ml (5 fl oz/⅔ cup) white wine
6 teaspoons Madeira
6 teaspoons chicken stock
2 teaspoons salt
1½ teaspoons ground black pepper
10 juniper berries, crushed
2 cloves garlic, crushed
6 bay leaves
bay leaves, orange slices and cranberries, to garnish

Preheat oven to 150C (300F/Gas 2). Remove skin from belly pork and rind and bone from bacon. Using a mincer fitted with a fine blade, mince pork, bacon, chicken and veal into a large bowl. Stir in wine, Madeira, chicken stock, salt, pepper, juniper berries and garlic. Mix together until thoroughly blended. Spoon mixture into a 1.75 litre (3 pint/7½ cup) ovenproof dish, press down firmly and arrange bay leaves on top. Cover dish with double thickness foil and stand dish in a roasting tin half-filled with cold water.

Cook in the oven for 1¾-2 hours until terrine feels firm in centre and shrinks from side of dish. Leave to become completely cold in dish. Replace bay leaves with fresh ones and garnish with orange slices and cranberries. Chill until required.

Serves 20.

Note: This terrine freezes successfully for up to 2 months.

POUSSIN NOËL

2 oven-ready poussins
4 rashers unsmoked streaky bacon
3 teaspoons plain flour
155 ml (5 fl oz/²⁄₃ cup) white wine
chicken stock
sprigs of herbs and apricot slices, to garnish

STUFFING: 15 g (½ oz/3 teaspoons) butter
1 shallot, finely chopped
8 dried apricots, chopped
6 teaspoons sweetcorn kernels
3 teaspoons chopped fresh sage, thyme and parsley
60 ml (2 fl oz/¼ cup) white wine
½ teaspoon salt
½ teaspoon ground black pepper

Preheat oven to 190C (375F/Gas 5). Put poussins in a small roasting tin. To make stuffing, melt butter in a saucepan, add shallot and cook until tender, stirring occasionally. Remove pan from heat, add apricots, sweetcorn, sage, thyme, parsley, white wine, salt and pepper. Stir until evenly mixed. Lift skin flap at neck end of poussins and fill each with some stuffing. Tuck flap under wing tips. Place remaining stuffing inside body cavities of poussins. Secure tail ends with skewers.

Cover breast and body of poussins with rashers of bacon. Cook in the oven for 1 hour or until meat is tender. Arrange poussins on a serving plate, remove bacon, chop finely and sprinkle over each poussin. Stir flour into juices in roasting tin; add white wine. Bring to boil, stirring, add a little stock, if necessary, to dilute gravy. Cook for 2 minutes, then pour into a serving dish. Garnish poussins with fresh herbs and slices of apricot.

Serves 2.

— TURKEY VEGETABLE STRUDEL —

9 leaves of filo or strudel pastry, thawed

SAUCE: 45 g (1½ oz/9 teaspoons) butter
45 g (1½ oz/¼ cup) plain flour
1 bay leaf
250 ml (8 fl oz/1 cup) milk
155 ml (5 fl oz/⅔ cup) single (light) cream
salt and ground black pepper

FILLING: 125 g (4 oz/½ cup) butter, melted
90 g (3 oz) leek, sliced
90 g (3 oz) fennel, thinly sliced
90 g (3 oz) button mushrooms, sliced
90 g (3oz/1 cup) sweetcorn kernels
4 teaspoons chopped fresh parsley
250 g (8 oz/1 cup) diced, cooked turkey

Cover filo pastry with a damp cloth to prevent it drying. Preheat oven to 220C (425F/Gas 7). To make sauce, put butter, flour, bay leaf and milk in a saucepan. Bring to boil, whisking until thick. Cook gently for 2 minutes, then stir in cream and salt and pepper. To make filling, place 6 teaspoons of butter in a frying pan, add leek, fennel and mushrooms and fry gently for 2-3 minutes. Stir in sweetcorn, parsley and turkey. Mix with the sauce and leave until cold.

Lay 3 sheets of filo pastry flat on a tea towel, brushing between each sheet with melted butter. Spread with ⅓ of filling to within 2.5 cm (1 in) of edges, repeat twice more using remaining pastry and filling. Fold in all edges, roll up neatly into a roll with aid of tea towel and roll onto a greaseproof paper-lined baking sheet. Brush with remaining butter and cook in the oven for 20-25 minutes until golden brown. Serve hot, cut into slices.

Serves 6.

FRUIT PORK PILLOWS

30 g (1 oz/6 teaspoons) butter
2 tenderloins pork, cut into 8 pieces
125 g (4 oz/1 cup) dried apricots, chopped
9 teaspoons whipping cream, whipped
500 g (1 lb) puff pastry, thawed if frozen
125 g (4 oz/⅔ cup) fresh or canned cherries, stoned
    and halved
8 fresh sage leaves
salt and black pepper
a little beaten egg
cherries and sage leaves, to garnish

Preheat oven to 200C (400F/Gas 6). Line a baking sheet with non-stick paper. Melt butter in a frying pan. Fry pork for 1 minute.

Drain and cool pork. In a bowl, mix together apricots and cream. Cut pastry into 8 pieces, roll out one piece very thinly and trim to a neat square, measuring about 10 cm (4 in). Spread ⅛ apricot filling over centre, top with 4 cherry halves, a sage leaf and a piece of pork. Season to taste with salt and pepper.

Brush pastry edges with beaten egg, fold pastry over pork and seal edges well. Invert onto baking sheet and brush with egg to glaze. Repeat to make another 7 parcels. Roll out and cut pastry trimmings into holly leaves, berries and thin pastry strips and use to decorate each parcel. Glaze with egg and bake in the oven for 20-30 minutes until pastry is risen and golden brown. Serve hot, garnished with cherries and sage leaves.

Serves 8.

TURKEY RISOTTO

60 g (2 oz/¼ cup) butter
1 large onion, sliced
1 clove garlic, crushed
125 g (4 oz) button mushrooms, sliced
185 g (6 oz/1 cup) Italian risotto rice
1 teaspoon saffron strands
1 teaspoon salt
½ teaspoon ground black pepper
470 ml (15 fl oz/1¾ cups) turkey stock
155 ml (5 fl oz/⅔ cup) white wine
1 small red pepper (capsicum)
1 small yellow pepper (capsicum)
315 g (10 oz) cooked turkey
30 g (1 oz/6 teaspoons) grated Gruyère cheese
3 teaspoons chopped fresh parsley

Melt butter in a flameproof dish or saucepan, add onion, garlic and mushrooms and cook for 2 minutes until tender. Stir in rice and cook for a further 2 minutes. Add saffron, salt, pepper, stock and wine, bring to boil, stirring, then cover and cook very gently for 15 minutes. Grill red and yellow peppers (capsicums) until skin has charred and peppers (capsicums) are tender. Remove stalks, seeds and skin and cut peppers (capsicums) into fine strips. Cut turkey into bite-sized pieces.

Add turkey and peppers (capsicums) to risotto, stir carefully to distribute ingredients, then cover and cook for a further 5 minutes until rice is tender and mixture is creamy, but not dry. Serve risotto in the flameproof dish or arrange on a warmed serving plate. Sprinkle with cheese and parsley and serve hot.

Serves 4-6.

TURKEY SOUP

1 turkey, chicken or goose carcass
90 g (3 oz/⅓ cup) butter
3 rashers streaky bacon, chopped
1 onion, chopped
2 carrots, chopped
3 sticks celery, chopped
2 leeks, sliced
60 g (2 oz/½ cup) plain flour
1 teaspoon salt
1 teaspoon ground black pepper
155 ml (5 fl oz/⅔ cup) sherry or wine
croûtons and chopped fresh parsley, to garnish

Preheat oven to 220C (425F/Gas 7). Break up carcass, reserving any pieces of meat.

Place carcass in a roasting tin with skin and any leftover bones. Cook in the oven for 45-50 minutes until bones are golden brown. Melt 30 g (1 oz/6 teaspoons) butter in a large saucepan; add bacon, onion, carrots, celery and leeks. Fry quickly until vegetables are lightly browned, stirring frequently. Add carcass and enough cold water to cover all ingredients. Bring to boil, cover and cook very gently for 2-3 hours.

Strain stock into a large bowl, and allow to cool, or leave overnight. Remove fat from top of mixture. Melt remaining butter in a saucepan, stir in flour and cook for 1 minute, stirring. Gradually add stock, bring to boil, stirring, and cook for 5 minutes. Add salt and pepper, sherry or wine and reserved turkey pieces and heat through for 2-3 minutes. Serve hot, garnished with croûtons and chopped parsley.

Serves 6.

CLEMENTINE DUCK

2.5 kg (5 lb) oven-ready duck with giblets
salt
30 g (1 oz/6 teaspoons) butter
3 shallots, finely chopped
315 ml (10 fl oz/1¼ cups) rosé wine
½ teaspoon ground black pepper
1 teaspoon wholegrain mustard
3 teaspoons chopped fresh oregano
finely grated peel and juice of 2 clementines
6 teaspoons redcurrant jelly
90 g (3 oz/¾ cup) redcurrants, thawed
1 egg, beaten
90 g (3 oz/1½ cups) soft white breadcrumbs
clementine wedges, redcurrants and oregano sprigs, to
    garnish

Preheat oven to 220C (425F/Gas 7). Remove duck giblets; reserve liver and chop. Prick skin all over with a fork and rub with salt. Place duck in a roasting tin. Cook in oven for 45 minutes until golden; cool for 15 minutes. Remove duck and strain fat from roasting tin. Melt butter in a pan, add shallots and liver and fry quickly, stirring, until shallots are tender. Add wine, salt, pepper and mustard; boil for 5 minutes. Mix into roasting tin; strain back into pan. Add the oregano, the grated clementine peel and juice and redcurrant jelly.

Cut off leg and wing joints from duck. Cut breast into thin slices and arrange in a warm ovenproof dish. Pour over sauce, add redcurrants, cover dish; keep warm. Brush duck joints with egg, coat with breadcrumbs and arrange in a roasting tin. Return to oven for 20-30 minutes until golden brown. Arrange on a serving dish with breast meat and sauce. Garnish with clementine wedges, redcurrants and oregano sprigs.

Serves 4.

— VEGETABLE TURKEY KEBABS —

6 teaspoons almond oil
½ teaspoon salt
½ teaspoon ground black pepper
1 teaspoon Dijon mustard
2 teaspoons clear honey
3 teaspoons chopped fresh rosemary
3 teaspoons raspberry vinegar
250 g (8 oz) cooked turkey breast
3 small courgettes (zucchini)
1 corn-on-the-cob, thawed if frozen
8 cherry tomatoes
8 rashers streaky bacon

In a bowl, put oil, salt, pepper, mustard, honey, rosemary and vinegar. Beat well.

Cut turkey into even, bite-sized pieces; slice courgettes (zucchini) and corn into thick slices, and remove calyx from tomatoes. Add turkey and vegetables to marinade, stir well to coat evenly, cover with plastic wrap and leave in a cool place for at least 1 hour. Remove rinds and bones from bacon, stretch rashers flat with a knife and cut each rasher into 3. Remove turkey pieces from marinade and wrap each piece in a strip of bacon.

Using 4 fine, long, wooden kebab skewers, thread a mixture of ingredients onto each one. Brush well with marinade and arrange on a grill rack lined with foil. Cook under a hot grill for 5-6 minutes, turning frequently until bacon is crisp and vegetables are just tender. Serve immediately.

Serves 4.

POLANAISE CRUMBLE

250 g (8 oz) cauliflower flowerets
250 g (8 oz) broccoli flowerets

TOPPING: 30 g (1 oz/6 teaspoons) butter
60 g (2 oz/1 cup) soft white breadcrumbs
3 teaspoons chopped fresh parsley
1 hard-boiled egg, sieved

SAUCE: 30 g (1 oz/6 teaspoons) butter
30 g (1 oz/¼ cup) plain flour
315 ml (10 fl oz/1¼ cups) milk
salt and ground black pepper

To make topping, heat butter in a pan, add breadcrumbs and fry until golden. Put in a bowl; add parsley and egg.

To make sauce, put butter, flour, milk and salt and pepper to taste in a saucepan. Whisk together over a moderate heat until thick. Cook for 1-2 minutes, then keep warm.

Cook cauliflower and broccoli in boiling, salted water for 3-4 minutes until just tender. Drain and place in a warmed serving dish. Pour over sauce and sprinkle over topping. Serve hot.

Serves 4-6.

– ALMOND BRUSSELS SPROUTS –

500 g (1 lb) small Brussels sprouts
30 g (1 oz/6 teaspoons) butter
30 g (1 oz/¼ cup) flaked almonds
1 clove garlic, crushed
1 teaspoon finely grated lemon peel
1 teaspoon lemon juice
½ teaspoon salt
½ teaspoon ground black pepper
lemon twists and herb sprigs, to garnish

Trim stalks off sprouts and make a cut across each one. Cook in boiling, salted water for 4-5 minutes until just tender. Drain well and place in a warmed serving dish.

Meanwhile, melt butter in a small frying pan, add flaked almonds and garlic and fry until almonds are golden brown. Stir in lemon peel and juice and salt and pepper. Mix well.

Sprinkle almond mixture over sprouts and stir gently to mix. Serve immediately, garnished with lemon twists and herb sprigs.

Serves 4.

SOUFFLÉ POTATOES

4 large potatoes
30 g (1 oz/6 teaspoons) butter
6 teaspoons single (light) cream
1 teaspoon salt
½ teaspoon ground black pepper
½ teaspoon grated nutmeg
2 eggs, separated

Preheat oven to 220C (425F/Gas 7). Scrub potato skins and remove any 'eyes'. Pierce each potato several times using a small, sharp knife, and arrange on a baking sheet. Cook in the oven for 1 hour, or until potatoes are tender.

Cut each potato in half, carefully scoop out the potato flesh and place in a bowl or an electric mixer fitted with a beater. Replace potato skins on a baking sheet and cook in the oven for 10-15 minutes until crisp and golden. Meanwhile mash or beat potato until smooth, add butter, cream, salt, pepper, nutmeg and egg yolks. Mash or beat until thoroughly blended.

Stiffly whisk egg whites, add to potato and fold in gently, using a spatula, until evenly mixed. Fill each potato skin with mixture and return to oven for 10-15 minutes or until risen and lightly browned. Serve immediately.

Serves 8.

Variations: Add 125 g (4 oz) chopped crispy bacon or grated cheese to filling for a change, or add chopped mixed herbs to taste.

—CREAMED SPINACH & CELERY—

1 kg (2 lb) spinach
6 sticks celery
30 g (1 oz/6 teaspoons) butter
1 teaspoon grated nutmeg
90 ml (3 fl oz/⅓ cup) double (thick) cream
¼ teaspoon salt
½ teaspoon ground black pepper

Stem and wash spinach; wash and thinly slice celery. Cook celery and spinach separately in boiling, salted water until just tender. Drain each vegetable thoroughly, pressing out excess water from spinach.

Line bases and sides of 8 warmed individual soufflé dishes with a few whole spinach leaves. Chop remaining spinach roughly. Melt butter in a saucepan, add nutmeg, cream and salt and pepper and bring to the boil. Add spinach and toss well.

Half-fill each soufflé dish with spinach mixture, cover each with a layer of celery, reserving a little for garnish, and fill each up to the top with remaining spinach. Press firmly. Just before serving, invert spinach moulds onto a serving plate and garnish with reserved celery slices. Serve warm.

Serves 8.

BAKED POTATO LAYER

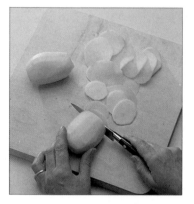

1 kg (2 lb) medium potatoes
30 g (1 oz/6 teaspoons) butter
1 clove garlic, crushed
1 teaspoon salt
1 teaspoon ground black pepper
125 g (4 oz/1 cup) grated Cheddar cheese
315 ml (10 fl oz/1¼ cups) milk
155 ml (5 fl oz/⅔ cup) single (light) cream
1 large egg, beaten
parsley sprigs, to garnish

Preheat oven to 190C (375F/Gas 5). Peel and very thinly slice potatoes. Using ½ the butter, lightly grease a 22.5 cm (9 in) shallow ovenproof dish.

Arrange a layer of potato slices over base and up sides of the dish. Sprinkle with some of the garlic, salt, pepper and cheese. Continue to layer until all these ingredients have been used, finishing with a layer of potatoes and a sprinkling of cheese.

Place milk, cream and egg in a bowl and whisk until smooth. Pour over potato layer and dot with remaining butter. Cook in the oven for 1 hour until golden brown and potatoes are tender. Garnish with parsley sprigs and serve hot.

Serves 4-6.

—GLAZED CARROTS & ONIONS—

12 small, even-sized carrots
16 pickling onions
1 teaspoon salt
60 ml (2 fl oz/¼ cup) turkey or chicken stock
3 teaspoons caster sugar
30 g (1 oz/6 teaspoons) butter
3 teaspoons chopped fresh parsley
herb sprigs, to garnish

Peel and trim carrots to make them even in size, if necessary. Peel and trim onions. Cook carrots and onions separately in boiling, salted water for 5-8 minutes until just tender. Drain well.

Place stock, sugar and butter in a saucepan and heat gently, stirring until sugar has dissolved and butter has melted. Boil rapidly until mixture is reduced by half.

Add carrots, onions and parsley and toss well until thoroughly coated in glaze. Arrange on a warmed serving dish and serve immediately, garnished with sprigs of herbs.

Serves 4.

—ROUND CHRISTMAS PUDDING—

500 g (1 lb/3 cups) mixed dried fruit
60 g (2 oz/½ cup) chopped prunes
45 g (1½ oz/⅓ cup) chopped glacé cherries
60 g (2 oz/½ cup) chopped almonds
45 g (1½ oz/¼ cup) grated carrot
45 g (1½ oz/¼ cup) grated cooking apple
finely grated peel and juice of 1 orange
3 teaspoons black treacle (molasses)
90 ml (3 fl oz/⅓ cup) stout
3 teaspoons brandy plus extra for serving
1 egg
60 g (2 oz/¼ cup) butter, melted
60 g (2 oz/⅓ cup) dark soft brown sugar
¾ teaspoon ground allspice
60 g (2 oz/½ cup) plain flour
60 g (2 oz/1 cup) soft white breadcrumbs

In a large mixing bowl, put mixed fruit, prunes, cherries, almonds, carrot, apple, orange peel and juice, treacle, stout and the brandy. Mix well together. Stir in egg, butter, sugar, allspice, flour and breadcrumbs until well blended. Cover; leave in a cool place until ready to cook. Use a buttered round Christmas pudding mould, measuring 12.5 cm (5 in) in diameter, or a rice steaming mould, lined with double thickness foil. Fill each half of mould with mixture. Place two halves together, securing mould tightly.

Half-fill a saucepan with water, bring to the boil and place mould carefully into pan so that water comes just below join of mould. Cover and cook very gently for 6 hours. Cool in mould; turn out and wrap in foil until required. To re-heat pudding: unwrap and replace in mould. Cook as before for 2-3 hours. Turn onto a serving plate, decorate with holly, spoon over warmed brandy and set alight. Serve with Brandy Butter, see opposite.

Serves 8.

BRANDY BUTTER

185 g (6 oz/¾ cup) unsalted butter
185 g (6 oz/¾ cup) caster sugar
90 ml (3 fl oz/⅓ cup) brandy

Put butter in a bowl or food processor fitted with a metal blade. Beat or process butter until white and creamy. Add sugar and beat or process until light and fluffy.

Add brandy, a drop at a time, beating continuously until enough has been added to well-flavour the butter. Take care the mixture does not curdle through overbeating.

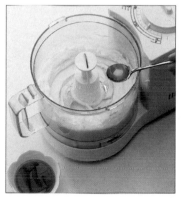

Pile butter into a glass dish and serve with a spoon, or, if preferred, spread the mixture about 1 cm (½ in) thick over a flat dish and leave to set hard. Using a fancy cutter, cut Brandy Butter into shapes and arrange in a serving dish.

Serves 8.

CHRISTMAS CAKE

1.15 kg (2¼ lb/6¾ cups) mixed dried fruit
185 g (6 oz/¾ cup) quartered glacé cherries
90 g (3oz/¾ cup) flaked almonds
finely grated peel and juice of 1 orange
125 ml (4 fl oz/½ cup) brandy or sherry
375 g (12 oz/3 cups) plain flour
3 teaspoons ground mixed spice
75 g (2½ oz/⅔ cup) ground almonds
280 g (9 oz/1½ cups) dark soft brown sugar
280 g (9 oz/1½ cups) butter, softened
6 teaspoons black treacle (molasses)
5 eggs
9 teaspoons apricot jam, boiled and sieved
875 g (1¾ lb) marzipan
1 kg (2 lb) ready-to-roll fondant icing
red and green food colourings

Preheat oven to 140C (275F/Gas 1). Line a
20 cm (8 in) square or 22.5 cm (9 in) round
cake tin with double thickness greased
greaseproof paper. Tie a double thickness
band of brown paper around tin and stand tin
on double thickness lined baking sheet. Place
dried fruit, cherries and almonds in a large
bowl; stir until well mixed. Add orange peel
and juice and brandy or sherry; mix well
together.

In another bowl, put flour, spice, ground almonds, sugar, butter, treacle (molasses) and eggs. Stir all ingredients together using a wooden spoon to mix, then beat until smooth and glossy. Add fruit mixture to cake mixture; stir until evenly mixed.

Spoon mixture into prepared tin, level top with back of metal spoon, making a slight depression in centre. Cook in the oven for 3¼-3½ hours or until a skewer inserted in the centre comes out clean. Leave cake in tin to cool; turn out, remove paper and place on a cake board.

Brush top and side of cake with apricot jam. Knead marzipan, roll out to 0.5 cm (¼ in) thickness and use to cover top and sides of cake; trim to fit neatly at base. Roll out fondant icing on a lightly-sugared surface and use to cover cake; press icing over top and down side of cake. Trim off excess icing at base.

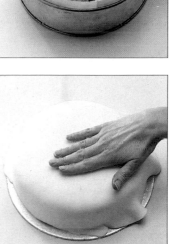

Knead icing trimmings together; colour ⅓ red and remainder green with food colourings. Make tiny berries with some of the red icing; roll and cut out holly leaves from green icing, mark leaf veins with a knife and leave decorations to set. Arrange on top of cake, securing with jam. Cut out 'NOEL' from red icing and place on cake. Tie ribbon around outside of cake. Leave cake to dry overnight.

Makes 30 slices.

FESTIVE MINCE PIES

375 g (12 oz/3 cups) plain flour
185 g (6 oz/¾ cup) butter
6 teaspoons caster sugar
1 egg, separated
375 g (12 oz/1½ cups) mincemeat
red and green food colourings

Preheat oven to 200C (400F/Gas 6). Sift flour into a bowl. Add butter and rub in finely with the fingers until mixture resembles breadcrumbs. Using a fork, stir in sugar, egg yolk and enough cold water to mix to a soft dough. Knead gently on a lightly floured surface.

Roll out pastry thinly and cut out twenty 7.5 cm (3 in) rounds and twenty 5 cm (2 in) rounds. Line 20 tartlet tins with the larger pastry circles, prick base of each with a fork and half-fill with mincemeat. Brush edges of each pastry lid with water, invert and press on top of tart to seal edges. Pierce a hole in centre of each lid to allow steam to escape. Roll out pastry trimmings thinly and using a holly leaf cutter, cut out 40 holly leaves and mark leaf veins with a knife. Roll tiny balls of pastry to form berries.

Brush top of each mince pie with egg white and arrange holly leaves and berries on top. Bake in the oven for 15 minutes until cooked, but pale. Divide remaining egg white between 2 cups; colour one red and the other green with food colourings. Brush leaves with green glaze and berries with red glaze. Bake in the oven for a further 5 minutes. Cool on wire rack.

Makes 20.

— SOUTHERN COMFORT CAKE —

315 g (10 oz/1¼ cups) butter
10 tablespoons golden syrup
315 ml (10 fl oz/1¼ cups) Southern Comfort
finely grated peel and juice of 1 orange
finely grated peel and juice of 1 lemon
1.15 kg (2¼ lb/6¼ cups) mixed dried fruit
315 g (10 oz/2½ cups) dried apricots, chopped
315 g (10 oz/2¼ cups) dried dates, chopped
¾ teaspoon bicarbonate of soda
3 eggs
500 g (1 lb/3½ cups) wholemeal self-raising flour
2 teaspoons ground allspice
125 ml (4 fl oz/½ cup) apricot jam
250 g (8 oz/2¼ cups) assorted nuts
apricots and dates, to decorate

Preheat oven to 150C (300F/Gas 2). Grease and double-line a 25 x 20 cm (10 x 8 in), 5 cm (2 in) deep, oblong tin with greaseproof paper. Place tin on a double-lined baking sheet. In a large saucepan, place butter, golden syrup, Southern Comfort, orange and lemon peels and juices. Heat until almost boiling. Add mixed fruit, apricots and dates; stir until well blended and leave until almost cold. Add bicarbonate of soda, eggs, flour and allspice and stir until mixture is thoroughly mixed.

Spoon mixture into tin, level top; bake in the oven for 2¼-2½ hours or until a skewer inserted in the centre comes out clean. Cool in tin, then turn out and wrap in foil until required. Boil and sieve apricot jam. Cut cake into 6 pieces, brush with apricot jam, arrange nuts and fruit over top; glaze with remaining jam. Leave until set, then wrap in plastic wrap or cellophane and tie with ribbon.

Makes 6 individual cakes.

— MINI CHRISTMAS CAKES —

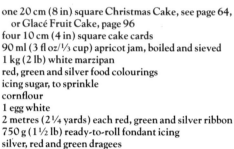

one 20 cm (8 in) square Christmas Cake, see page 64,
  or Glacé Fruit Cake, page 96
four 10 cm (4 in) square cake cards
90 ml (3 fl oz/⅓ cup) apricot jam, boiled and sieved
1 kg (2 lb) white marzipan
red, green and silver food colourings
icing sugar, to sprinkle
cornflour
1 egg white
2 metres (2¼ yards) each red, green and silver ribbon
750 g (1½ lb) ready-to-roll fondant icing
silver, red and green dragees
red and green cake candles

Cut cake into 4 small square cakes, place
each on a cake card and brush evenly with
apricot jam. Cut marzipan into 4 pieces;
colour one piece pale pink and one pale green
with food colourings. Roll out one piece at a
time on a lightly sugared surface, to about a
15 cm (6 in) square. Place over cake, trim to
fit; reserve marzipan trimmings. Leave the
two white marzipan cakes in a warm place to
dry. Using a crimper dipped in cornflour,
crimp top and bottom edge of pink and green
cakes.

Colour remaining green and pink marzipan
bright green and red by adding a few more
drops of food colouring. Roll out green
marzipan thinly and cut out about 20 holly
leaves using a holly leaf cutter, and shape red
marzipan into tiny holly berries. Arrange
holly leaves and berries over top of coloured
cakes, securing each with some egg white.
Measure and cut ribbons to fit round outside
of each cake.

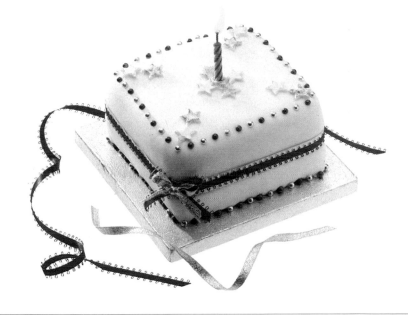

Sprinkle work surface with icing sugar, cut icing in half; place half in a polythene bag and seal. Knead remaining icing until smooth, roll out to a 20 cm (8 in) square. Place over white cake, smooth top and sides with well-cornfloured hands and trim off excess icing around base of cake. Repeat to cover second cake. Knead icing trimmings together.

Press silver and red dragees around top edge and base of cake; secure with egg white, if necessary. Repeat with green and silver dragees on remaining cake. Tie silver and green and silver and red ribbon on each respective cake; tie with pretty bows.

Roll out icing trimmings on a surface lightly sprinkled with cornflour and cut out 26 stars using a tiny star-shaped cutter. Using food colourings, paint surfaces of 14 stars silver, 6 stars red and 6 stars green. Leave to dry. Arrange green and 7 silver stars on green and silver cake, and red and 7 silver stars on red and silver cake. Place a candle in centre of each. Leave to dry. Put each cake into a pretty box and tie with ribbon.

Makes 4 individual cakes.

MOBILES

155 g (5 oz/1¼ cups) plain flour
30 g (1 oz/9 teaspoons) custard powder
90 g (3 oz/⅓ cup) butter
45 g (1½ oz/8 teaspoons) caster sugar
1 egg white
6 teaspoons lemon juice
250 g (8 oz) clear fruit sweets
125 g (4 oz) white chocolate, melted
red and green oil-based, or powdered, food colourings
red and green ribbon

Preheat oven to 180C (350F/Gas 4). Line 2 baking sheets with non-stick baking paper. Sift flour and custard powder into a bowl.

Rub in butter finely. Stir in sugar, egg white and enough lemon juice to form a soft dough. Knead lightly; roll out to 0.5 cm (¼ in) thickness. Using a 5 cm (2 in) biscuit cutter, cut out 20 shapes; put on baking sheets, spaced apart. Using a sharp knife or small cutters, cut out centres, leaving a 1 cm (½ in) frame. Make a hole at top of each. Put ½ a sweet into centres. Bake in the oven until sweets have melted. Cool on sheets.

Divide chocolate between 3 bowls. Colour one red and one green using food colourings. When chocolate has set enough to leave a trail on surface, fill 3 greaseproof paper piping bags with the mixtures, fold down tops and snip off points. Decorate biscuits with swirls, dots and lines of coloured chocolate. When set, peel off paper, thread different lengths of ribbon through holes and hang up near the light so that the coloured centres shine.

Makes 20.

SMOKED TROUT PÂTÉ

125 g (4 oz) thinly sliced smoked salmon trout
60 g (2 oz/1 cup) soft white breadcrumbs
375 g (12 oz) smoked trout, filleted
125 g (4 oz/½ cup) low-fat soft cheese
60 g (2 oz/¼ cup) unsalted butter, melted
½ teaspoon ground black pepper
1 teaspoon finely grated lemon peel
9 teaspoons sherry or brandy
3 teaspoons chopped fresh dill
3 teaspoons chopped fresh tarragon
lemon twists and dill sprigs, to garnish

Line base and sides of a 500 g (1 lb) loaf tin with plastic wrap.

Trim smoked salmon trout to fit base and sides of tin neatly. Alternatively, line 8 individual soufflé dishes. Using a food processor fitted with a metal blade, add breadcrumbs, trout, cheese, butter, pepper, lemon peel, sherry or brandy, chopped dill and tarragon. Process until smooth. Alternatively, beat all ingredients together in a bowl.

Spoon pâté mixture into lined tin; press down firmly and level. Cover top with plastic wrap and place in refrigerator until firm. Remove plastic wrap. Invert pâté onto a serving plate, remove remaining plastic wrap and garnish with lemon twists and dill. Cut into thin slices.

Serves 8.

FLAVOURED CHEESES

PORT & PEPPERCORN CHEESE

125 g (4 oz/½ cup) low-fat soft cheese
90 g (3 oz/¾ cup) grated Cheddar cheese
6 teaspoons ruby port
chives and 2 teaspoons pink peppercorns, to garnish

Put soft cheese, Cheddar cheese and port in a bowl; mix well with a wooden spoon until evenly blended. Shape into a round ball, then press into a disc shape. Garnish with a lattice of chives and a border of pink peppercorns. Chill.

BLUE CHEESE

125 g (4 oz/½ cup) cream cheese
90 g (3 oz/¾ cup) grated blue Stilton cheese
1 teaspoon Dijon mustard
¼ teaspoon cayenne pepper
30 g (1 oz/¼ cup) sunflower seeds
30 g (1 oz/¼ cup) chopped walnuts

Put cream cheese, Stilton, mustard and cayenne in a bowl; mix well until evenly blended. Divide mixture in half; mould each into a cylinder shape. Roll one in sunflower seeds and one in walnuts. Chill.

HERBED CHEESE

125 g (4 oz/½ cup) full fat soft cheese
1 small clove garlic, crushed
2 teaspoons chopped fresh chives
1 teaspoon each chopped fresh oregano and thyme
¼ teaspoon ground black pepper
bay leaves and green peppercorns, to garnish

Mix ⅓ cheese with garlic, herbs and pepper; flatten into a ball. Flatten plain cheese and press around herbed ball. Garnish with bay leaves and peppercorns. Chill.

Makes 4 cheeses.

— PICKLED MIXED VEGETABLES —

1 cucumber, peeled
8 courgettes (zucchini), trimmed
500 g (1 lb) pickling onions, peeled
500 g (1lb) red and green peppers (capsicums), seeded
500 g (1 lb) green or red tomatoes, skinned and seeded
9 teaspoons salt

SPICED VINEGAR: 315 g (10 oz/2 cups) light soft brown
    sugar
1 teaspoon celery seeds
1 teaspoon ground turmeric
1 teaspoon ground mace
4 teaspoons mustard seeds
625 ml (20 fl oz/2½ cups) tarragon, cider or wine
    vinegar

Cut all vegetables into thin slices and arrange in a large bowl, sprinkling salt between each layer. Cover with plastic wrap and leave in a cool place for 3 hours. Drain vegetables and rinse thoroughly under running water; leave to drain thoroughly.

To make spiced vinegar, place all ingredients in a stainless steel or enamel saucepan and stir over a gentle heat until sugar has dissolved; boil for 3 minutes. Add vegetables to vinegar, bring to boil, stirring occasionally. Cook for 1 minute. Spoon vegetables into clean hot jars until packed tightly. Fill to top with vinegar mixture and seal immediately with vinegar-proof, airtight lids.

Makes 2.5 kg (5 lb).

— GINGER MARRONS GLACÉS —

PAVLOVA: **3 egg whites**
220 g (7 oz/1 cup) caster sugar
1 teaspoon white wine vinegar
1 teaspoon orange flower water
1 teaspoon cornflour

FILLING: **315 ml (10 fl oz/1¼ cups) whipping cream**
3 pieces preserved stem ginger in syrup
vanilla ice cream
10 whole marrons glacés, each cut into 8 pieces

Preheat oven to 140C (275F/Gas 1). Line 3 baking sheets with non-stick baking paper, mark ten 8 cm (3 in) circles and invert paper.

Whisk egg whites in a bowl until stiff. Gradually add sugar, whisking well after each addition until thick. In a bowl, blend together the vinegar, orange flower water and cornflour. Add to meringue and whisk until very thick and glossy. Place meringue in a large piping bag fitted with a small star nozzle. Pipe a shell edging around the marked lines on the paper, then fill in centres with a thin layer of meringue. Pipe a second shell edging on top of the first edge.

Bake in the oven for 45 minutes. Turn off oven and leave in oven to cool. Remove when cold; store in an airtight container until required. Whip cream in a bowl until thick, place ½ in a piping bag fitted with a nozzle. Chop the ginger and fold into remaining cream and spread over each pavlova. Just before serving, top each with scoops of ice cream, whipped cream and a marron glacé.

Serves 10.

—SOUFFLÉ LIME & CHOC LAYER—

4 eggs, separated
90 g (3 oz/⅓ cup) caster sugar
3 teaspoons powdered gelatine
finely grated peel and juice of 1 lime
60 g (2 oz) plain (dark) chocolate, melted
315 ml (10 fl oz/1¼ cups) whipping cream
chocolate curls and lime peel, to decorate

Place egg yolks and sugar in a bowl over a saucepan of simmering water. Whisk until pale and thick. Remove bowl from saucepan, continue to whisk until mixture leaves a trail when whisk is lifted.

Sprinkle gelatine over 9 teaspoons water in a small bowl and leave to soften for 2-3 minutes. Stand bowl in a saucepan of hot water and stir until dissolved and quite hot. Stir gelatine into mixture until well blended. Pour ½ quantity of mixture into another bowl. Stir lime peel and juice into one mixture and chocolate into remaining mixture. Stir each until well blended. Whisk egg whites in a bowl until stiff. Whip cream until thick.

Add ½ quantity egg whites and cream to each mixture and fold in carefully until evenly blended. Spoon alternate spoonfuls of each mixture into 8 small glasses. Leave until set, then decorate with chocolate curls and lime peel.

Serves 8.

ROSE CUSTARD CREAMS

315 ml (10 fl oz/1¼ cups) milk
315 ml (10 fl oz/1¼ cups) double (thick) cream
2 eggs
2 egg yolks
30 g (1 oz/5 teaspoons) caster sugar
8 teaspoons rose water

MARINATED FRUIT: 4 teaspoons rose water
4 teaspoons rosé wine
8 teaspoons icing sugar
petals from 2 scented roses
125 g (4 oz) strawberries, sliced
125 g (4 oz) raspberries, thawed if frozen
1 star fruit, sliced

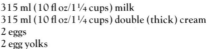

Preheat oven to 150C (300F/Gas 2). Place milk and cream in a saucepan and bring almost to boiling point. Beat eggs and yolks together in a bowl, then pour milk mixture onto eggs, stirring well. Add sugar and rose water and stir until well blended. Divide mixture between 8 individual soufflé dishes. Stand dishes in a roasting tin half-filled with cold water. Cook in the oven for about 1 hour until custard has set. Remove dishes from water and leave until cold.

To make marinated fruit, mix together rose water, wine, icing sugar and rose petals in a bowl. Add the fruit and stir until well mixed. Cover with plastic wrap and chill until ready to serve. Turn custards out onto individual plates and spoon marinated fruit around base of each one.

Serves 8.

TIPSY FRUIT JELLY

3 lemons
125 g (4 oz/½ cup) caster sugar
155 ml (5 fl oz/⅔ cup) claret
22 g (¾ oz/6 teaspoons) powdered gelatine
12 teaspoons hot water
375 g (12 oz) mixed fruit (grapes, lychees, pineapple and clementines)
whipped cream, to decorate

Using a potato peeler or sharp knife, pare the peel from lemons; squeeze out juice. Place peel in a saucepan with 315 ml (10 fl oz/1¼ cups) water and bring to boil. Add sugar; stir until dissolved.

Leave the mixture until cold, then strain into a measuring jug; stir in the lemon juice. Pour ⅓ lemon mixture into a bowl, add claret and stir until blended. Sprinkle gelatine over hot water in a small bowl; leave to soften. Stand bowl in a saucepan of hot water, stir until dissolved and quite hot. Add ½ gelatine to claret mixture, stirring well, and the remainder to lemon mixture, stirring well. Halve grapes and lychees, remove seeds and stones. Peel and slice pineapple and clementines.

Arrange ¼ of mixed fruit in base of 6 individual moulds or glasses. Spoon enough lemon jelly over fruit to cover. Leave to set. Arrange a second layer of fruit over set jelly layer and cover with claret jelly; leave to set. Repeat to make another lemon fruit layer and claret fruit layer. When jelly has set firm, turn out of moulds by dipping quickly into hand-hot water and inverting onto a plate, or serve in glasses, if preferred. Decorate with whipped cream.

Makes 6.

— AMARETTI CHEESE WHIP —

60 g (2 oz/¼ cup) caster sugar
2 eggs, separated
315 g (10 oz/1¼ cups) mascarpone cream cheese
finely grated peel of 1 tangerine
125 g (4 oz) mixed glacé fruit, chopped
30 g (1 oz) Amaretti biscuits
4 teaspoons Amaretti liqueur
155 ml (5 fl oz/⅔ cup) double (thick) cream
chopped glacé fruit and Amaretti biscuits, to decorate

Place sugar and egg yolks in a bowl over a saucepan of simmering water and whisk until mixture leaves a trail when whisk is lifted.

Stir in mascarpone cheese, tangerine peel and glacé fruit. Break Amaretti biscuits into pieces and add to mixture; stir in liqueur. Whisk egg whites in a bowl until stiff. Place cream in another bowl and whip until thick. Add egg whites and cream to cream cheese mixture and fold in carefully until mixture is evenly blended. Cover with plastic wrap and chill until required.

Just before serving, divide mixture between 6-8 small glasses and decorate with chopped glacé fruit and Amaretti biscuits.

Serves 6-8.

— LYCHEE & PORT ICE CREAM —

125 g (4 oz/½ cup) caster sugar
155 ml (5 fl oz/⅔ cup) ruby port
20 fresh lychees or 470 g (15 oz) can lychees
4 teaspoons fresh lime juice
315 ml (10 fl oz/1¼ cups) double (thick) cream
fresh or canned lychees and lime peel twists, to decorate

Place sugar and port in a saucepan and heat gently, stirring until sugar has dissolved. Peel lychees and remove stones, or drain canned lychees. Add lychees to port, bring to the boil, then cover and cook very gently for 2 minutes. Leave until cold.

Put port and lychees into a food processor fitted with a metal blade and process until smooth. Pour mixture into a sieve over a bowl and rub mixture through sieve using a wooden spoon. Stir in lime juice. Whip cream in a bowl until thick, add port mixture and fold in until evenly blended. Pour mixture into a plastic container, cover and freeze for 1-2 hours until mixture is almost frozen but still mushy.

Return mixture to processor and process until smooth and creamy. Return mixture to plastic container and freeze until firm. Scoop ice cream into serving dishes and decorate with lychees and lime peel.

Serves 6.

FROSTIE FRUIT BRULÉES

2 oranges
2 eating apples
2 figs
2 bananas, sliced
125 g (4 oz) grapes, seeded
6 teaspoons Marsala
625 ml (20 fl oz/2½ cups) double (thick) cream
185 g (6 oz/¾ cup) caster sugar
60 ml (2 fl oz/¼ cup) boiling water

Using a sharp knife, cut orange peel and pith away from flesh. Cut between membranes to remove segments. Quarter and core apples; slice thinly. Cut figs into thin wedges.

Mix all the fruit gently together in a bowl with Marsala. Divide fruit between 6 individual dishes. Place cream in a bowl and whip until very thick. Spoon cream evenly over the fruit. Chill until ready to serve.

Place sugar and water in a saucepan and heat gently, stirring occasionally, until sugar has dissolved. Boil rapidly until syrup turns a golden brown colour. Allow bubbles to subside, then drizzle caramel over top of fruit and cream. Serve immediately.

Serves 6.

FESTIVE CHEESECAKE

BASE: 60 g (2 oz/¼ cup) butter
3 teaspoons golden syrup
220 g (7 oz/2 cups) plain biscuit crumbs

FILLING AND TOPPING: 375 g (12 oz/1½ cups) cream
   cheese
155 ml (5 fl oz/⅔ cup) fromage frais
2 eggs, separated
4 teaspoons grenadine syrup
90 ml (3 fl oz/⅓ cup) Marsala
5 teaspoons powdered gelatine
1 star fruit, sliced
2 figs, sliced
10 kumquats, sliced
12 melon balls
10 green and black grapes, halved and seeded

Gently heat butter and syrup in a saucepan until melted. Stir in biscuit crumbs and press onto base of a 22.5 cm (9 in) spring-form tin. In a bowl, beat cream cheese, fromage frais, egg yolks, 3 teaspoons grenadine syrup and 6 teaspoons Marsala until smooth. Sprinkle gelatine over 9 teaspoons water in a small bowl; leave to soften. Stand bowl in saucepan of hot water and stir until dissolved and quite hot. Stir into cheese mixture and leave until thickened. Stiffly whisk egg whites; fold into mixture.

Pour into tin, shake to level; chill until set. In a bowl, place prepared fruit. Heat remaining grenadine and Marsala in a saucepan until hot, but not boiling. Pour over fruits and leave until cold. Drain liquor into a saucepan and arrange fruit over top of cheesecake. Boil liquid until syrupy and brush over fruit to glaze. Serve cut into slices.

Serves 8.

— CHOCOLATE CHERRY SLICE —

185 g (6 oz) plain (dark) chocolate
4 eggs
60 g (2 oz/¼ cup) caster sugar
45 g (1½ oz/¼ cup) plain flour

FILLING: 220 g (7 oz/1 cup) unsweetened marron purée
125 g (4 oz) plain (dark) chocolate, melted
315 ml (10 fl oz/1¼ cups) double (thick) cream
9 teaspoons Morello cherry jam
185 g (6 oz/1 cup) fresh or canned cherries, stoned and
  halved

Preheat oven to 190C (375F/Gas 5). Line a
32.5 x 22.5 cm (13 x 9 in) Swiss roll tin with
non-stick paper.

Melt chocolate in a bowl over a pan of hand-
hot water. Whisk eggs and sugar until pale
and thick enough to leave a trail. Stir in
chocolate; sift in flour and fold in gently.
Transfer to tin, shake to level and bake in the
oven for 20-25 minutes until firm to touch.
Cover with a damp tea towel; leave until
cold. To make filling, put marron purée and
chocolate in a food processor fitted with a
metal blade. Process until puréed. Fold in ⅔
cream. Stiffly whip remaining cream; place in
a piping bag fitted with a small star nozzle.

Turn cake out of tin; remove paper. Trim
edges and cut into 3 short strips across width.
Spread 2 strips of cake with jam, then cover
with ⅓ marron mixture. Arrange ⅓ cherry
halves on each; stack layers together on a
serving plate with remaining cake layer on
top. Spread top and sides with remaining
marron mixture and pipe cream around top
edge. Decorate with remaining cherry
halves. Chill.

Serves 10.

ENGLISH TRIFLE

1 egg, plus 2 egg yolks
30 g (1 oz/5 teaspoons) caster sugar
315 ml (10 fl oz/1¼ cups) milk
few drops vanilla essence
20 sponge fingers
6 teaspoons Madeira
3 teaspoons brandy
6 teaspoons raspberry jam
250 g (8 oz/1½ cups) raspberries, thawed if frozen
315 ml (10 fl oz/1¼ cups) double (thick) cream
16 ratafias and angelica leaves, to decorate

In a bowl, whisk egg, egg yolks and sugar until well blended. Bring milk and vanilla essence to the boil in a saucepan; pour onto eggs in bowl, stirring thoroughly. Rinse out saucepan and strain custard back into saucepan. Stirring continously, cook over a gentle heat until thick, but do not boil. Leave until cold. Dip one sponge finger at a time into Madeira and brandy mixed together, spread with some jam and sandwich together with another dipped sponge finger. Place in a glass dish.

Repeat with remaining sponge fingers, Madeira, brandy and jam to cover base of dish. Pour remaining Madeira and brandy over top; cover with ⅔ raspberries. In a bowl, whip cream until softly peaking and fold ⅔ into cold custard. Pour over sponges and raspberries in bowl. Place remaining cream in a piping bag fitted with a star nozzle. Decorate trifle with piped cream, ratafias, angelica leaves and remaining raspberries. Chill.

Serves 8.

— WHITE & PLAIN CHOC POTS —

125 g (4 oz) white chocolate
125 g (4 oz) plain (dark) chocolate
4 eggs, separated
3 teaspoons rum
3 teaspoons Cointreau
spirals of orange peel, to decorate, if desired

Break up each type of chocolate and place in separate bowls, each over a saucepan of hand-hot water. Stir occasionally until melted and smooth. Stir 2 egg yolks into each, then add rum to dark chocolate and Cointreau to white chocolate; stir until evenly blended.

In a bowl, stiffly whisk egg whites, then add ½ quantity to each of the chocolate mixtures. Fold in carefully until each mixture is evenly blended and smooth.

Place alternate spoonfuls of each mixture into 8 small glasses, or individual dishes. Leave in a cool place to set. Decorate with spirals of orange peel, if desired.

Makes 8.

FESTIVE MERINGUES

MERINGUE: **2 egg whites**
125 g (4 oz/½ cup) caster sugar

TOPPING: **250 g (8 oz) mixed glacé fruit, chopped**
8 teaspoons Strega liqueur
250 ml (8 fl oz/1 cup) double (thick) cream
60 ml (2 fl oz/¼ cup) Greek yogurt
1 star fruit, thinly sliced, to decorate

Preheat oven to 110C (225F/Gas ¼). Line 2 baking sheets with non-stick paper. Draw 10 oval shapes on each, using a 6 cm (2½ in) oval cutter. Invert paper.

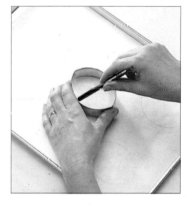

In a bowl, whisk egg whites until stiff. Whisk in sugar a little at a time, whisking thoroughly until thick. Place mixture in a large piping bag fitted with a medium star nozzle. Pipe shells of meringue around each oval shape, then fill in centres, making sure there are no gaps. Bake in the oven for 1½-2 hours until meringues are dry and crisp; lift off paper. Cool and store in an airtight tin until required.

In a bowl, mix fruit with Strega; cover and leave until required. Whip cream and yogurt together in a bowl until thick, add ⅔ of glacé fruit and all the liqueur and fold in until just mixed. Spoon mixture onto each meringue oval and decorate with slices of star fruit and remaining glacé fruit.

Makes 20.

–SAUCY CHOCOLATE PUDDINGS–

90 g (3 oz) white chocolate
90 g (3 oz) milk chocolate
90 g (3 oz) plain (dark) chocolate
3 egg yolks
2 teaspoons finely grated grapefruit peel
2 teaspoons grapefruit juice
3 teaspoons Southern Comfort
3 teaspoons ginger wine
185 g (6 oz/¾ cup) softened butter
155 ml (5 fl oz/⅔ cup) double (thick) cream
9 teaspoons fromage frais

GRAPEFRUIT SAUCE: finely grated peel and juice of 1
   grapefruit
2 teaspoons cornflour
3 teaspoons caster sugar

Break up chocolates and place in separate bowls, each over a saucepan of hand-hot water until melted. Stir an egg yolk into each. Add grapefruit peel and juice to white chocolate; Southern Comfort to plain (dark) chocolate and ginger wine to milk chocolate; stir until smooth. Leave to cool. Beat butter until light and fluffy; whip cream and fromage frais until thick. Fold ⅓ of each into the chocolate mixtures. Line 6 dariole moulds with plastic wrap. Divide milk chocolate mixture between moulds.

Repeat with a white chocolate layer and finally a dark chocolate layer. Tap moulds to level and freeze until firm or until required. To make sauce, make grapefruit juice and peel up to 185 ml (6 fl oz/¾ cup) with water. Blend with cornflour and sugar in a small saucepan. Bring to boil, stirring; cook for 30 seconds; cool. Invert moulds onto serving dishes 20 minutes before serving. Serve the puddings with the cold sauce.

Makes 6.

KUMQUAT CRANBERRY TARTS

WALNUT PASTRY: 185 g (6 oz/1½ cups) plain flour
125 g (4 oz/½ cup) butter
60 g (2 oz/½ cup) chopped walnuts
60 g (2 oz/¼ cup) caster sugar
1 egg, beaten

FILLING: 185 g (6 oz/¾ cup) caster sugar
250 g (8 oz) kumquats, sliced
250 g (8 oz/1½ cups) cranberries
185 g (6 oz/¾ cup) cream cheese
90 ml (3 fl oz/⅓ cup) Greek yogurt
1 teaspoon arrowroot

To make pastry, sift the flour into a bowl.

Add butter and rub in to form breadcrumbs.
Stir in walnuts, sugar and enough egg to form
a soft dough. Knead and roll out to line six 12
cm (4½ in) fluted flan tins. Trim edges and
prick bases; chill 30 minutes. Preheat oven to
190C (375F/Gas 5). Heat sugar and 250 ml
(8 fl oz/1 cup) water until dissolved. Bring to
boil, add kumquats; cook for 3 minutes.
Strain; return ⅓ syrup to pan; reserve
remaining syrup. Add cranberries to syrup in
pan, bring to boil, cover and cook for 3
minutes.

Strain, keeping individual syrups and fruit
separate. Bake tart cases in oven for 10-15
minutes until lightly browned. Cool. Beat
cream cheese with yogurt. Spread over base
of tarts. Arrange alternate circles of fruit in
tarts. Blend ½ teaspoon arrowroot into each
syrup; bring each to boil. Glaze kumquats
with clear syrup and cranberries with red
syrup. Leave to set.

Serves 6.

TIPSY FRUIT FOOL

500 g (1 lb) cooking apples, peeled and sliced
185 g (6 oz/2¼ cups) pre-soaked dried apricots
60 g (2 oz/¼ cup) caster sugar
pared peel and juice of 3 satsumas
6 teaspoons apricot brandy
90 ml (3 fl oz/⅓ cup) fromage frais
chocolate curls, to decorate, if desired

In a saucepan, place apples, apricots, sugar, satsuma peel and juice. Bring to boil, cover and cook until apples and apricots are tender. Remove satsuma peel, reserve some for decoration. Leave until cold.

Pour cold apple and apricot mixture into a food processor fitted with a metal blade. Process until puréed. Add apricot brandy and fromage frais and process until well blended. Divide mixture between individual glasses and chill until required.

Using a sharp knife, cut reserved satsuma peel into needle shreds or thin strips and use to decorate top of each dessert, adding a few chocolate curls, if desired.

Serves 6.

MANDARIN FIG SORBET

125 g (4 oz/½ cup) caster sugar
pared peel and juice of 4 mandarins
6 green figs
2 teaspoons powdered gelatine
2 egg whites
fig slices and mint sprigs, to decorate

Heat sugar and 155 ml (5 fl oz/⅔ cup) water in a saucepan, stirring occasionally until dissolved. Add mandarin peel and figs, bring to boil, then cover and simmer for 10 minutes. Leave until cold.

Remove mandarin peel and pour liquid and figs into a food processor and process until puréed. Sieve mixture. Sprinkle gelatine over 9 teaspoons water in a small bowl and leave to soften for 2-3 minutes. Stand bowl in a saucepan of hot water and stir until dissolved and quite hot. Add to fig purée with mandarin juice; stir well. Pour into a plastic container, cover and freeze for 2 hours or until partially frozen but still mushy.

Spoon mixture into a food processor and process until creamy, well blended and smooth. Stiffly whisk egg whites and fold into mixture. Return mixture to container, cover and freeze until firm, or until required. Place container of sorbet in refrigerator for 15 minutes to soften slightly before serving in scoops. Decorate with fig slices and mint.

Serves 6.

— COFFEE CHIFFON DESSERTS —

60 g (2 oz/¼ cup) butter
9 teaspoons golden syrup
220 g (7 oz/2 cups) crunchy oat biscuit crumbs

FILLING: 30 g (1 oz/9 teaspoons) cornflour
60 g (2 oz/¼ cup) caster sugar
3 teaspoons instant coffee
315 ml (10 fl oz/1¼ cups) milk
2 eggs, separated
5 teaspoons powdered gelatine
315 ml (10 fl oz/1¼ cups) whipping cream
155 ml (5 fl oz/⅔ cup) double (thick) cream, whipped
and liqueur chocolate coffee beans, to decorate

Melt butter and syrup in a saucepan; mix in biscuit crumbs. Divide between 8 tiny moulds, lined with plastic wrap; press evenly over bases and sides. Chill. Blend cornflour with sugar, coffee and milk in a saucepan. Bring to boil, stirring; cook for 2 minutes. Remove from heat; beat in egg yolks. Sprinkle gelatine over 9 teaspoons hot water in a small bowl; leave to soften. Stand bowl in a pan of hot water; stir until dissolved. Stir into coffee mixture; leave until thick but not set.

Stiffly whisk egg whites; whip cream until thick. Fold cream and egg whites evenly into coffee mixture. Divide mixture between the moulds, filling each to the top. Cover and chill until set. To serve, invert moulds onto serving plates and remove plastic wrap. Place remaining cream in a piping bag fitted with a star nozzle and pipe around top and base of moulds. Decorate with coffee beans.

Makes 8.

–AMARETTI MERINGUE BOMBES–

30 g (1 oz/6 teaspoons) butter, melted
20 Amaretti biscuits, crushed finely
375 g (12 oz) raspberries, thawed if frozen
4 teaspoons icing sugar
raspberries and Amaretti biscuits, to decorate

FILLING: 125 g (4 oz/2 cups) roughly crushed
   meringues
30 g (1 oz/¼ cup) Amaretti biscuits, broken into small
   pieces
60 g (2 oz/¼ cup) maraschino cherries, chopped
30 g (1 oz/¼ cup) chocolate dots (chips)
625 ml (20 fl oz/2½ cups) double (thick) cream

Brush 8 tiny moulds with melted butter.

Divide crushed Amaretti biscuits between moulds and shake well to coat evenly. Chill. To make filling, mix together meringues, Amaretti biscuits, cherries and chocolate in a bowl. Stir well. Whip cream until softly peaking, add meringue mixture and fold in very gently until evenly mixed. Fill each mould with meringue mixture, pressing well down to pack evenly. Cover and freeze until required.

Put raspberries and icing sugar in a food processor fitted with a metal blade and process until puréed. Sieve raspberry mixture into a jug. Just before serving, dip moulds into hand-hot water and invert onto serving plates. Decorate with a few raspberries and Amaretti biscuits and serve with raspberry sauce.

Makes 8.

— LIME & TANGERINE GÂTEAU —

12 trifle sponges
155 ml (5 fl oz/²⁄₃ cup) double (thick) cream
9 teaspoons fromage frais
25 g (1 oz/¼ cup) chopped pistachio nuts
lime and tangerine wedges, to decorate

FILLING: 3 eggs, separated
250 g (8 oz/1 cup) curd cheese
125 g (4 oz/½ cup) caster sugar
finely grated peel and juice of 2 tangerines
finely grated peel and juice of 2 limes
5 teaspoons powdered gelatine

To make filling, put egg yolks, curd cheese and sugar in a bowl. Beat until smooth.

Stir in fruit peels and ½ of juices. Sprinkle gelatine over 9 teaspoons water in a bowl; leave to soften. Stand bowl in a pan of hot water; stir until dissolved. Stir into cheese mixture; leave until thick. Line a 17.5 cm (7 in) square tin with plastic wrap. Cut sponges into 3 thin layers; line base and sides of tin. Sprinkle with ⅓ of remaining fruit juice. Stiffly whisk egg whites; fold into cheese mixture. Pour ½ into tin, cover with a layer of sponge; sprinkle with ⅓ juice.

Top with remaining sponge and juice. Cover with plastic wrap and chill until set. Turn gâteau onto a serving plate; remove plastic wrap. Whip cream and fromage frais until thick, place ¼ in a piping bag fitted with a small star nozzle. Spread remaining cream over gâteau; press pistachio nuts onto sides. Pipe a border around top and base of gâteau. Decorate with lime and tangerine wedges.

Serves 12.

PLUM & APPLE KUCHEN

315 g (10 oz) packet white bread mix
185 ml (6 fl oz/¾ cup) warm water
30 g (1 oz/6 teaspoons) butter, melted
90 g (3 oz/¾ cup) ground almonds
60 g (2 oz/¼ cup) caster sugar
1 teaspoon ground mixed spice
500 g (1 lb) cooking apples, peeled, cored and sliced
1 kg (2 lb) plums, stoned and halved
90 ml (3 fl oz/⅓ cup) plum jam, boiled and sieved
3 teaspoons flaked almonds

Preheat oven to 220C (425F/Gas 7). Place bread mix in a bowl.

Add warm water according to instructions on packet. Knead dough until smooth; cover and leave for 5 minutes. Re-knead dough and roll out to a 30 cm (12 in) round on a lightly floured surface. Place in a buttered 25 cm (10 in) flan tin, or on a baking sheet, and brush dough with butter. In a bowl, mix together ground almonds, sugar and mixed spice. Sprinkle over dough.

Arrange apple slices and plum halves neatly over almond mixture. Bake in the oven for 20-30 minutes until dough is well risen and filling is tender. Cool on a wire rack, then brush with plum jam to glaze, and sprinkle with flaked almonds.

Serves 12.

RUM TRUFFLE CAKE

220 g (7 oz) plain (dark) chocolate
125 g (4 oz/½ cup) unsalted butter
75 ml (2½ fl oz/⅓ cup) dark rum
3 eggs, separated
125 g (4 oz/½ cup) caster sugar
90 g (3 oz/¾ cup) plain flour
60 g (2 oz/½ cup) ground almonds

ICING: 220 g (7 oz) plain (dark) chocolate
315 ml (10 fl oz/1¼ cups) double (thick) cream
3 teaspoons dark rum
60 g (2 oz) white chocolate, grated

Butter and flour a 20 cm (8 in) round cake tin and line base with greaseproof paper.

Preheat oven to 180C (350F/Gas 4). Place chocolate and butter in a bowl over a saucepan of hand-hot water. Stir occasionally until melted. Add rum and stir well.

Place egg yolks and sugar in a bowl over a saucepan of simmering water. Whisk until thick and pale, remove bowl from pan and continue to whisk until mixture leaves a trail when whisk is lifted. Stir in chocolate mixture until evenly blended. Mix together flour and ground almonds, add to mixture and fold in carefully using a spatula.

Whisk egg whites until stiff, fold in ⅓ at a time until all egg white has been incorporated. Pour mixture into tin and bake in the oven for 45-55 minutes until firm to touch in centre. Turn out of tin and cool on a wire rack.

To make the icing, melt 125 g (4 oz) of the chocolate with 60 ml (2 fl oz/¼ cup) cream in a bowl over a pan of hot water. Stir in rum until well blended. Leave to cool. Whip 125 ml (4 fl oz/½ cup) cream in a bowl until thick, add ½ chocolate rum mixture and fold in to make a smooth icing.

Cut cake in half, sandwich together with the chocolate icing and spread remainder over top and sides. Chill cake and remaining ½ of chocolate rum mixture until firm. Melt remaining chocolate and cream in a bowl, stir until smooth; cool and pour mixture over cake to cover evenly. Shape firmed chocolate rum mixture into 16 truffles, coat in grated white chocolate. Arrange on top of cake; chill to set.

Makes 10-12 slices.

GLACÉ FRUIT CAKE

315 g (10 oz) mixed glacé fruit,
  chopped
125 g (4 oz/1 cup) dried apricots, chopped
125 g (4 oz/1 cup) chopped pecan nuts
finely grated peel and juice of 1 lemon
375 g (12 oz/3 cups) plain flour
1 teaspoon baking powder
1 ½ teaspoons ground mixed spice
185 g (6 oz/1⅔ cups) ground almonds
375 g (12 oz/1¾ cups) caster sugar
375 g (12 oz/1½ cups) butter, softened
4 eggs

TOPPING: 60 ml (2 fl oz/¼ cup) apricot jam
mixed glacé fruit and nuts
sprig of fresh holly

Line a 20 cm (8 in) square cake tin, or a 22.5 cm (9 in) round tin, with double thickness greased greaseproof paper. Tie a double thickness band of brown paper around tin and stand tin on double thickness lined baking sheet. Preheat oven to 140C (275F/Gas 1). Mix glacé fruit with apricots, nuts, lemon peel and juice; stir. Sift flour, baking powder and mixed spice into a bowl, add almonds, sugar, butter and eggs. Mix, then beat for 2 minutes. Stir in fruit and nuts.

Put in tin; smooth top. Bake in oven for 2¼-2½ hours, or until the cake feels firm and springy when pressed in centre. Cool in tin; turn out and wrap in foil. Place jam and 2 teaspoons water in a pan, bring to boil, stirring; sieve. Brush top of cake with glaze, arrange fruit and nuts over top; brush with remaining glaze. Leave to set, tie with ribbon. Decorate with holly.

Makes 30 slices.

TINY CHOCOLATE LOGS

3 eggs
45 g (1½ oz/8 teaspoons) caster sugar
30 g (1 oz/¼ cup) plain flour
3 teaspoons cocoa

FILLING AND DECORATION: 315 ml (10 fl oz/1¼ cups)
    double (thick) cream
125 g (4 oz) plain (dark) chocolate
marzipan toadstools

Preheat oven to 200C (400F/Gas 6). Line a
30 cm (12 in) baking tray (with edges) with
non-stick baking paper. Place eggs and sugar
in a bowl over a saucepan of simmering water
and whisk until thick and pale.

Remove bowl from saucepan, continue
whisking until mixture leaves a trail when
whisk is lifted. Sift flour and cocoa onto
surface of mixture and fold in carefully until
mixture is evenly blended. Pour mixture onto
baking tray and spread out carefully to edges.
Bake in the oven for 8-10 minutes, or until
firm to touch. Cool slightly, turn out and
remove paper, then trim edges and cut in half
lengthwise. Place 60 ml (2 fl oz/¼ cup) cream
in a bowl with chocolate. Place over a pan of
hot water; stir until melted. Whip remaining
cream until almost thick.

When chocolate has cooled, fold it carefully
into whipped cream. Using ⅓ chocolate
cream, spread over each strip of sponge. Roll
each into a firm roll from the long edge. Wrap
in plastic wrap and chill until firm. Cut each
roll into 6 lengths, spread each with
remaining chocolate cream, mark cream into
lines. Decorate with marzipan toadstools.
Keep the rolls cool until ready to serve.

Makes 12.

— CHOCOLATE CIGARETTES —

2 egg whites
100 g (3½ oz/⅓ cup plus 3 teaspoons) caster sugar
52 g (1¾ oz/¼ cup plus 9 teaspoons) plain flour
2 teaspoons cocoa
60 g (2 oz/¼ cup) unsalted butter, melted
60 g (2 oz) white chocolate, melted

Preheat oven to 200C (400F/Gas 6). Line 2 baking sheets with non-stick baking paper. Place egg whites in a bowl and whisk until stiff. Add caster sugar gradually, whisking well after each addition. Sift flour and cocoa over surface of mixture, add butter and fold in carefully until mixture is evenly blended.

Place 3 spoonfuls of mixture onto each baking sheet, well spaced apart. Spread each into a thin round. Bake, one sheet at a time, in the oven for 3-4 minutes, loosen each round with a palette knife, then return to the oven for 1 minute.

Take out one chocolate round at a time and quickly roll around a greased chopstick, or wooden spoon handle, to form a tube. Slip off and cool cigarette on a wire rack. Repeat with remaining rounds. Cook second tray of mixture, then repeat to make about 25 cigarettes. Dip both ends of each cigarette into melted chocolate. Leave to set on a paper-lined baking sheet. Store in an airtight container until required.

Makes 25.

– CRÈME DE MENTHE BISCUITS –

250 g (8 oz) plain (dark) chocolate
30 g (1 oz/6 teaspoons) butter
220 g (7 oz/2 cups) digestive biscuit crumbs
90 g (3 oz/¾ cup) plain cake crumbs
caster sugar for sprinkling

FILLING: 60 g (2 oz/¼ cup) unsalted butter
125 g (4 oz/¾ cup) icing sugar, sieved
2 teaspoons crème de menthe

Make filling first. Place butter in a bowl and beat with a wooden spoon until soft and smooth. Gradually beat in icing sugar and crème de menthe until light and fluffy.

Break up chocolate and place in a bowl. Add butter and place over a saucepan of hand-hot water. Stir occasionally until melted. Add biscuit and cake crumbs and stir until evenly mixed and mixture forms a ball. Sprinkle a 25 cm (10 in) square of foil with caster sugar.

Roll out chocolate mixture on the foil to a 20 cm (8 in) square. Spread crème de menthe mixture evenly over chocolate square to within 1 cm (½ in) of edges. Roll up carefully into a neat roll using the foil to help. Wrap in foil and chill until firm. Cut into thin slices as and when required.

Makes 20 slices.

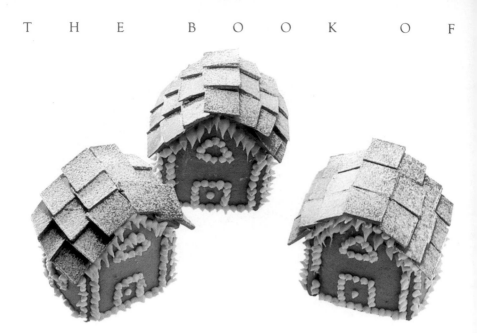

GINGERBREAD HOUSES

6 teaspoons golden syrup
6 teaspoons black treacle (molasses)
30 g (1 oz/6 teaspoons) light soft brown sugar
60 g (2 oz/¼ cup) butter
185 g (6 oz/1½ cups) plain flour
1½ teaspoons ground ginger
½ teaspoon bicarbonate of soda
1 egg, beaten

DECORATION: 125 g (4 oz) white chocolate
125 g (4 oz) plain (dark) chocolate
pink, green and yellow food colourings
icing sugar for dusting

Preheat oven to 200C (400F/Gas 6). Line 2 baking sheets with non-stick baking paper. Put syrup, treacle (molasses), sugar and butter in a saucepan. Heat gently, stirring occasionally, until melted.

Sift flour and ginger into a bowl. Stir bicarbonate of soda into melted mixture, add to flour with enough beaten egg to mix to form a soft dough. Knead on a lightly floured surface until smooth and free from cracks. Cut off ⅓ dough; wrap in plastic wrap.

Roll out remaining ⅔ dough thinly and cut out thirty-two 4 cm (1½ in) squares of dough and place, spaced apart, on a baking sheet. Roll out remaining dough and cut out sixteen 6 x 4 cm (2½ x 1½ in) oblongs. Measure and mark 2.5 cm (1 in) down side of each oblong. Cut from each mark to centre of oblong to shape a 'pitch' for 'roof'. Place on baking sheet and bake in the oven for 8-10 minutes until golden brown. Cool on wire rack.

Break up and place white and plain (dark) chocolate in separate bowls over hand-hot water. Stir occasionally until melted. Divide white chocolate between 3 small bowls and colour pink, green and yellow with food colourings. Assemble each house using plain (dark) chocolate to stick 2 side and 2 end walls together and 2 roof pieces in position; leave to set. Spread remaining plain (dark) chocolate over non-stick baking paper.

When almost set, invert onto another piece of paper, peel off baking paper and cut chocolate into 2 cm (¾ in) squares for roof tiles. Secure tiles onto roof with melted chocolate, starting at base of each roof and working to top. Using coloured chocolate, fill 3 greaseproof paper piping bags, snip off points and pipe in doors, windows and coloured beads down all the joins. Leave to set. Dust with icing sugar.

Makes 8.

ADVENT BISCUITS

BISCUIT DOUGH: 155 g (5 oz/1¼ cups) plain flour
90 g (3 oz/⅓ cup) butter
30 g (1 oz/¼ cup) ground almonds
45 g (1½ oz/8 teaspoons) caster sugar
1 egg yolk

DECORATION: 1 egg white
250 g (8 oz/1½ cups) icing sugar, sifted
red, green, yellow and black food colouring pens

Preheat oven to 180C (350F/Gas 4). Lightly
flour 2 baking sheets. Sift flour into a bowl;
rub in butter finely.

Stir in ground almonds, sugar, egg yolk and
enough cold water to form a soft dough.
Knead dough on a lightly floured surface, roll
out thinly and cut out 24 squares, rounds or
ovals using a 5.5 cm (2¼ in) cutter. Arrange
on baking sheets and make a hole in top of
each biscuit with a drinking straw. Bake in
the oven for 10-15 minutes until lightly
browned at edges. Cool on wire rack.

Place egg white in a bowl, stir in enough icing
sugar to mix to the consistency of thick
cream. Beat until smooth and glossy. Dip
surface of each biscuit into icing to cover
evenly; allow excess to fall away. Place on
rack to dry. When dry and hard, use food
colouring pens to number biscuits 1 to 24 and
draw a design or message on each biscuit.
Thread biscuits with ribbons and hang one up
each day from 1st to 24th December.

Makes 24.

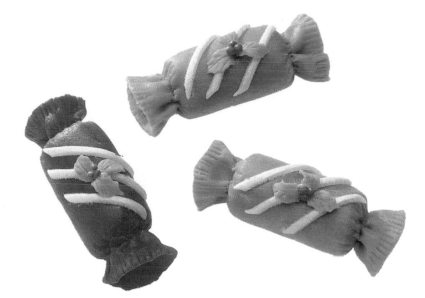

CHRISTMAS CRACKERS

2 eggs
50 g (2 oz/¼ cup) caster sugar
50 g (2 oz/½ cup) plain flour
caster sugar for sprinkling
125 ml (4 fl oz/½ cup) apricot jam, boiled and sieved

DECORATION· **500 g (1 lb) white marzipan**
red, green and gold food colourings

Preheat oven to 190C (375F/Gas 5). Line base and sides of a 32.5 x 22.5 cm (13 x 9 in) Swiss roll tin with greased greaseproof paper. Place eggs and sugar in a heatproof bowl over a saucepan of simmering water.

Whisk mixture until thick and pale. Remove from pan, whisk until cool and thick enough to leave a trail. Sift flour onto surface and fold in lightly. Pour into tin; bake in oven for 10-15 minutes until well risen. Sprinkle greaseproof paper with sugar, invert cake, peel off paper; trim edges. Cut cake in half lengthwise, spread jam to within 1 cm (½ in) of edges. Roll up into 2 long thin rolls. Cool; cut into 12 rolls; brush with jam.

Reserve 60 g (2 oz) of the marzipan; halve remainder. Colour one piece red and one green with food colourings. Roll out green marzipan thinly and cut out six 11 x 10 cm (4½ x 4 in) oblongs. Roll up 6 cake rolls in marzipan with joins underneath, squeeze ends and flute like a cracker. Repeat with red marzipan. Use trimmings to make holly leaves and berries. Roll out remaining marzipan, trim crackers with strips; brush with gold colouring. Decorate with holly.

Makes 12.

CHRISTMAS GIFT CAKES

CAKE: 125 g (4 oz/1 cup) self-raising flour
1 teaspoon baking powder
60 g (2 oz/⅓ cup) hazelnuts, toasted and ground
185 g (6 oz/¾ cup) caster sugar
185 g (6 oz/¾ cup) butter, softened
3 eggs

DECORATION: 6 teaspoons apricot jam, boiled
   and sieved
625 g (1¼ lb) ready-to-roll fondant icing
red and green food colourings
icing sugar for sprinkling

Preheat oven to 170C (325F/Gas 3). Line base and sides of a 20 cm (8 in) square cake tin. Sift flour and baking powder into mixing bowl. Add hazelnuts, sugar, butter and eggs. Mix with a wooden spoon and beat for 1-2 minutes until smooth and glossy. Spoon mixture into tin, bake in the oven for 40-45 minutes until well risen and firm to touch. Cool in tin for 10 minutes, turn out, remove paper and cool on wire rack. When cold, cut into 25 squares and brush each with apricot jam.

Cut icing into 3 pieces; colour one piece red and one green. Cut a small piece off each portion and reserve. Roll out white icing thinly on a lightly sugared surface. Cut into eight 5 cm (2 in) squares. Cover 8 cakes with squares of white icing, tucking excess icing under bases. Repeat with remaining icing and cakes and cover 8 in red and 9 in green icing. Roll out reserved icing in thin lengths and trim cakes with 'ribbons and bows'. Leave to dry in a warm place.

Makes 25.

— MARASCHINO FRUIT RING —

125 g (4 oz/1 cup) wholemeal self-raising flour
125 g (4 oz/3/4 cup) light soft brown sugar
125 g (4 oz/1/2 cup) butter, softened
3 eggs
90 g (3 oz/1/2 cup) pecan nuts, chopped
90 g (3 oz/1/2 cup) raisins
90 g (3 oz/1/2 cup) red cocktail cherries
90 g (3 oz/1/2 cup) green glacé cherries

DECORATION: 90 g (3 oz/1/2 cup) icing sugar, sieved
8 teaspoons maraschino cherry syrup
6 red and 6 green cherries, sliced

Preheat oven to 150C (300F/Gas 2). Lightly oil a 22.5 cm (9 in) ring mould. Place flour, sugar, butter and eggs in a mixing bowl. Stir together until well mixed, then beat for 1-2 minutes until smooth and glossy. Add nuts, raisins and cherries to mixture and stir until evenly mixed. Spoon mixture into ring mould and level top. Bake in the oven for about 1 hour until cake feels firm to touch or until a skewer inserted in centre comes out clean.

Loosen edges of cake with a knife and cool in tin. Invert onto a wire rack. To decorate, put icing sugar in a bowl, stir in enough cherry syrup to mix to the consistency of thick cream. Spoon icing over cold cake, arrange sliced cherries in clusters around top of cake. Leave to set.

Serves 10.

— SCOTTISH BLACK BUN —

315 g (10 oz) packet white bread mix
1 egg yolk
purple and green food colourings

FILLING: 250 g (8 oz/1 cup) mixed dried fruit
30 g (1 oz/¼ cup) chopped glacé cherries
30 g (1 oz/¼ cup) chopped flaked almonds
finely grated peel and juice of 1 orange
30 g (1 oz/6 teaspoons) light soft brown sugar
60 g (2 oz/¼ cup) butter, melted
60 g (2 oz/½ cup) plain flour
1 teaspoon ground allspice
1 egg, beaten

Make up bread mix as directed on packet.

Knead for 5 minutes, place in a polythene bag and leave until filling has been made. Preheat oven to 180C (350F/Gas 4). Lightly flour 2 baking sheets. To make filling, put dried fruit, cherries, almonds and orange peel and juice in a mixing bowl. Mix together with a wooden spoon. Add sugar, butter, flour, allspice and whole egg and stir well until all ingredients are evenly mixed.

Knead dough on a lightly floured surface and cut into 11 pieces. Roll out thinly, one piece at a time, to a 10 cm (4 in) round; reserve trimmings. Brush edge of round with water, place a heaped spoonful of filling in centre of dough.

Draw up edge of dough to cover filling, seal in centre and shape into a neat ball. Turn bun over with join underneath. Place on baking sheet. Repeat to make 10 in total. Prick buns all over with a fine skewer.

Roll out remaining dough very thinly; cut out 10 thistle shapes, stems and leaves. Brush each bun with 1 teaspoon of egg yolk mixed with a little water to glaze. Bake in the oven for 25 minutes, then remove from oven.

Divide remaining egg yolk in half, colour one half purple and one half green with food colourings. Brush thistles purple and leaves and stems green. Return to oven for a further 5 minutes until glaze has set and buns are golden brown. Cool on a wire rack.

Makes 10 buns.

SNOWY FLIP

4 eggs, separated
60 g (2 oz/¼ cup) caster sugar
315 ml (10 fl oz/1¼ cups) double (thick) cream
155 ml (5 fl oz/⅔ cup) milk, chilled
250 ml (8 fl oz/1 cup) whisky or brandy
soda water
1 teaspoon ground mace
twists of lemon and orange peel, to decorate

Put egg whites and egg yolks in separate bowls. Add ½ quantity sugar to yolks and whisk until pale and creamy. Wash beaters and whisk egg whites until stiff; add remaining sugar and whisk again until stiff.

Add egg whites to yolk mixture and fold in carefully until well mixed and foamy. Whip cream until softly peaking. Stir in milk and whisky or brandy. Cover with plastic wrap and chill until required.

Stir gently and pour into 8 tall glasses. Fill up glasses with soda water and sprinkle with mace. Decorate each one with a twist of lemon and orange peel.

Serves 8.

CHRISTMAS EVE MULL

1 bottle white wine
1 bottle red wine
315 ml (10 fl oz/1 ¼ cups) sweet red vermouth
3 teaspoons Angostura bitters
6 strips orange peel
8 whole cloves
1 cinnamon stick
8 cardamom pods, crushed
3 teaspoons raisins
125 g (4 oz/½ cup) caster sugar
lemon, lime, orange and apple slices, to decorate

Pour white and red wines into a large stainless steel or enamel saucepan.

Add vermouth, bitters, orange peel, cloves, cinnamon and cardamom pods. Heat wine mixture gently until very hot, but do not boil. Remove saucepan from heat, cover with a lid and allow to cool. Strain wine into a bowl.

Just before serving, return wine to a clean saucepan, add raisins and sugar. Heat gently until sugar has dissolved and wine is hot enough to drink. Decorate with fruit slices and serve in heatproof glasses or mugs.

Serves 18.

SOUCHON PUNCH

1 Lapsang Souchon tea bag
625 ml (20 fl oz/2½ cups) boiling water
4 teaspoons light soft brown sugar
315 ml (10 fl oz/1¼ cups) clear apple juice
90 ml (3 fl oz/⅓ cup) bourbon or brandy
2 lemon slices
3 lime slices
625 ml (20 fl oz/2½ cups) American dry ginger ale
ice cubes
lemon geranium leaves
lemon and lime peel spirals, to garnish

Place tea bag in a jug and pour on the boiling water.

Leave tea to infuse for 4-5 minutes without stirring, then remove tea bag. Stir in sugar and leave tea until cold. Pour tea into a large glass bowl, add apple juice, bourbon or brandy and lemon and lime slices.

Just before serving, add ginger ale, ice cubes and lemon geranium leaves. Stir well and serve garnished with spirals of lemon and lime peel.

Serves 12.

APPLE & ALE MULL

1 kg (2 lb) cooking apples
1 ¼ litres (40 fl oz/5 cups) ginger ale or ginger beer
6 whole cloves
1 blade of mace
1 teaspoon grated nutmeg
½ teaspoon ground ginger
3 strips orange peel
red and green apple slices and lemon slices, to decorate

Preheat oven to 200C (400F/Gas 6). Wash apples and remove stalks. Arrange on a baking sheet and cook in the oven for 30-40 minutes until soft.

Place apples in a saucepan and mash them. Add ginger ale or ginger beer, cloves, mace, nutmeg, ginger and orange peel. Bring to boil, remove from heat and leave until cool. Strain apple mixture through a nylon sieve into a bowl, pressing through as much apple as possible.

Just before serving, return apple and ale mixture to a clean saucepan and heat until hot enough to drink. Float red and green apple slices and lemon slices on top and serve in heatproof glasses or mugs.

Serves 8.

HOT BUTTERED RUM

4 cinnamon sticks
4 teaspoons light soft brown sugar
125 ml (4 fl oz/½ cup) dark rum
625 ml (20 fl oz/2½ cups) cider
30 g (1 oz/6 teaspoons) butter
1 teaspoon ground mace
4 lemon slices

Divide cinnamon sticks, sugar and rum between 4 warm, heatproof glasses or mugs.

Place cider in a saucepan and heat until very hot, but not boiling. Fill each glass or mug almost to the top with cider.

Add a knob of butter, a sprinkling of mace and a lemon slice to each glass or mug. Stir well and serve hot.

Serves 4.

ROSÉ GLOW

60 ml (2 fl oz/¼ cup) sweet red vermouth
60 ml (2 fl oz/¼ cup) cherry brandy
60 ml (2 fl oz/¼ cup) brandy
1 kiwi fruit, peeled and sliced
8 maraschino cherries, halved
orange, lemon or lime slices
1 bottle rosé wine
ice cubes
sprigs of mint and borage and rose petals, if desired, to
    decorate
1 bottle sparkling white wine

Pour vermouth, cherry brandy and brandy
into a large punch bowl.

Add kiwi fruit, cherries and orange, lemon or
lime slices. Stir to mix well. Just before
serving, pour in rosé wine and add ice cubes.
Decorate with mint, borage and rose petals, if
desired.

Add sparkling wine and serve at once in
punch glasses or cups, including some fruit
and ice with each serving.

Serves 10.

SNOWBALL FIZZ

125 g (4 oz) white chocolate
finely grated peel and juice of 2 limes
375 ml (12 fl oz/1½ cups) red or white grape juice
1 egg white
30 g (1 oz/5 teaspoons) caster sugar
soda or sparkling mineral water
1 teaspoon grated milk chocolate

Break up chocolate and place in a bowl over a saucepan of hand-hot water. Stir occasionally until melted and smooth. Stir in lime peel and juice.

Divide grape juice equally between 4 tall glasses, add ¼ of chocolate lime mixture to each and stir until well blended.

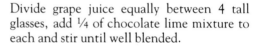

In a bowl, whisk egg white until stiff, add sugar, a little at a time, and whisk until thick. Just before serving, divide meringue between glasses and fill to the top with soda or sparkling water. Sprinkle with grated chocolate and serve at once.

Makes 4.

SUNRISE & SUNSET

90 ml (3 fl oz/⅓ cup) apricot nectar juice
90 ml (3 fl oz/⅓ cup) pineapple juice
155 ml (5 fl oz/⅔ cup) sparkling lemonade
155 ml (5 fl oz/⅔ cup) sparkling orange juice
4 teaspoons grenadine syrup
crushed ice
2 lemon slices
2 cocktail umbrellas
2 drinking straws

Using 2 goblets or tumblers, pour apricot nectar into one glass and pineapple juice into another glass. Add lemonade to apricot juice and sparkling orange to pineapple juice.

Carefully spoon 2 teaspoons grenadine syrup into each drink, allowing it to settle at the bottom of each glass.

Add a little crushed ice, a lemon slice and a cocktail umbrella to each glass. Serve each with a drinking straw.

Makes 2.

Note: Children will love these brightly coloured drinks. The pineapple drink is the sunrise and the apricot the sunset.

— FESTIVE DECORATIVE RINGS —

250 g (8 oz/2 cups) plain flour
½ teaspoon caster sugar
½ teaspoon salt
15 g (½ oz/3 teaspoons) butter
1 teaspoon easy-blend dried yeast
140 ml (4½ fl oz/½ cup) warm water
1 egg yolk, to glaze
red and green food colourings (optional)
festive ribbon

In a bowl, put sifted flour, sugar and salt. Add butter and rub in finely. Stir in yeast and enough warm water to form a soft dough. Knead on a lightly floured surface until smooth and no longer sticky.

Return dough to bowl, cover with plastic wrap and leave for 5 minutes. Re-knead dough until smooth. Cut off ¼ of dough and reserve. Shape remainder into a 60 cm (24 in) roll. Cut in half; shape into 2 rings by joining ends together. Seal well and place on a floured baking sheet. Cover and leave in a warm place to rise for 20-30 minutes. Meanwhile, roll out remaining dough very thinly and cut out about 40 holly leaves; shape 40 beads of dough into berries. Put on a floured plate, cover with plastic wrap and leave in a cool place.

Preheat oven to 220C (425F/Gas 7). Divide egg yolk between 3 egg cups, add 1 teaspoon water to one and brush over dough rings. Add red and green colourings separately to remaining egg yolk. Bake rings in the oven for 10-15 minutes until risen, but pale. Arrange leaves and berries around one or both rings, glaze leaves green and berries red. Return to oven for 5-6 minutes until glaze has set. Decorate with ribbon.

Makes 2 rings.

— CHOCOLATE DECORATIONS —

125 g (4 oz) plain (dark) chocolate
250 g (8 oz) white chocolate
pink, green and yellow oil-based, or powdered, food
   colourings
pink, green and yellow ribbon

Break up each chocolate and put in separate
bowls over saucepans of hand-hot water. Stir
occasionally until melted. Divide ½ white
chocolate between 3 bowls and colour pink,
green and yellow with food colourings.

To make novelty shapes, draw around biscuit
or cookie cutters on non-stick baking paper.
Invert paper and place on a baking sheet.
Half-fill 2 greaseproof paper piping bags with
melted plain (dark) chocolate. Snip a small
point off one bag and pipe a fine outline of
chocolate following the drawn shapes. Snip a
larger point off end of remaining piping bag
and pipe chocolate into shapes to give an
over-filled and rounded appearance.

Repeat to make different shaped chocolate
decorations, using white and some coloured
chocolate. Leave to set hard, then carefully
peel off paper, taking care not to mark
surfaces. Sandwich matching shapes together
with remaining melted chocolates, placing
ribbon loops in-between. Decorate shapes
with piped coloured chocolate using a
greaseproof paper piping bag. Allow all
decorations to dry before hanging up with
different coloured ribbons.

Makes about 20.

SUGAR CRYSTAL DECORATIONS

375 g (12 oz/1¾ cups) caster sugar
blue, pink, green and yellow food colourings
fine coloured ribbons

Place sugar in a bowl and add 3-4 teaspoons cold water, adding a little at a time and stirring with a fork until sugar is the consistency of damp sand. Divide sugar between 5 bowls; leave one white and tint remaining 4 mixtures pale blue, pink, green and yellow.

Using plastic Christmas decoration moulds, fill one shape at a time and press firmly to pack well. Place a loop of ribbon into mixture when mould is only half-filled, then fill to top and press down well. Fill with layers of different coloured sugars, if preferred. Repeat filling moulds with coloured sugars, place a piece of thick card over top of moulds and invert. Lift off moulds and leave shapes to dry in a warm place.

Fill larger moulds like bells, cones or half egg shells with sugar; pack well. Invert shapes onto a tray; leave until sugar has set, forming a crust. Return shapes to moulds, scoop out sugar from centre leaving a hollow shape. Make holes for ribbons with a skewer. Turn out of moulds and leave to dry. Thread with ribbon. Decorate or paint, using a fine paint brush and food colourings, or food colouring pens.

Makes about 25.

— SUGAR CHRISTMAS CARDS —

1 teaspoon powdered gelatine
1 teaspoon liquid glucose
1 teaspoon white fat
250 g (8 oz/1 ½ cups) icing sugar, sifted
½ teaspoon gum tragacanth
½ egg white
green and red food colourings and assorted food
    colouring pens
4 teaspoons ready-made royal icing

Sprinkle gelatine over 3 teaspoons cold water
in a small bowl and leave to soften for 2-3
minutes. Stand bowl in a saucepan of hot
water and stir until dissolved and quite hot.
Add glucose and fat; stir until melted.

Place icing sugar and gum tragacanth in a
bowl; add egg white and gelatine. Stir to form
a soft paste. Knead on an icing-sugared
surface until smooth. Keep sealed in a
polythene bag until required. Take 30 g (1 oz)
icing, roll out thinly, cut out two 7.5 cm (3
in) squares. Flute or scallop edges on 3 sides of
each piece. Cut out small rounds between
scalloped edges. Cut 2 evenly-spaced holes
on each plain edge. Dry on a flat surface,
sprinkled with cornflour, in a warm, dry place
overnight.

Colour trimmings with green and red food
colourings: make berries from red icing and
holly leaves from green icing; leave to dry.
Draw a design with food colouring pens and
write a message on inside of card. Thread
ribbon in and out of holes around the edge.
Thread two pieces of 'card' together with
ribbon and tie in a bow. Attach holly leaves
and berries on front of icing 'card' with a little
icing. Place in a pretty box and gift wrap.

Makes about 6 cards.

INDEX